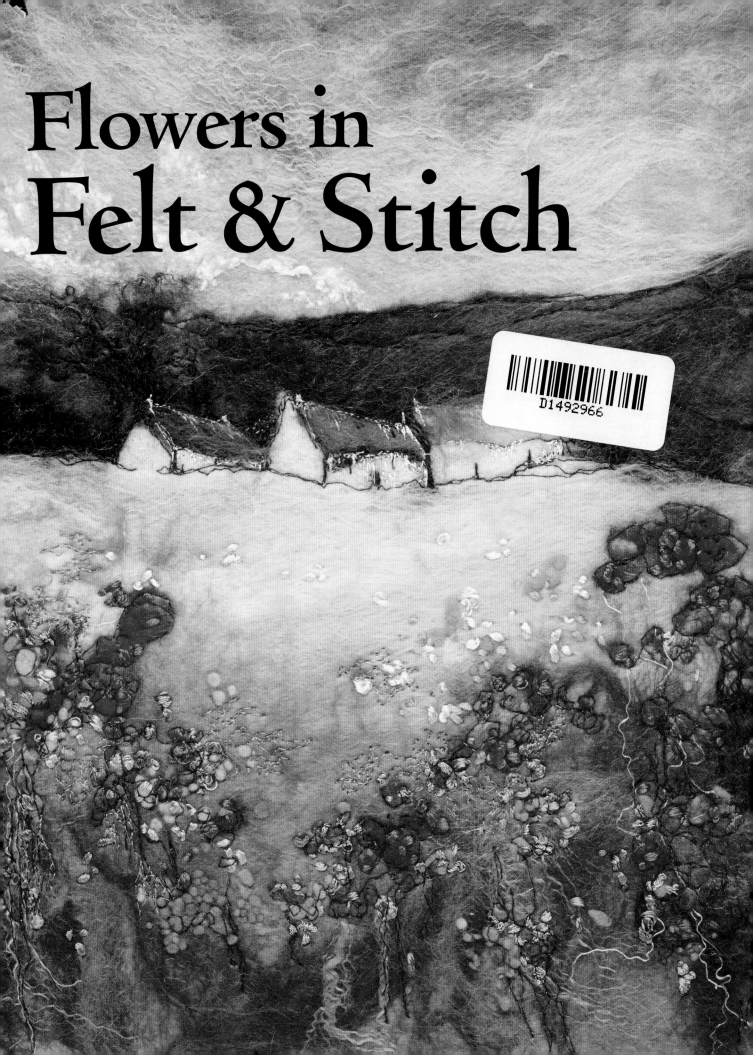

Flowers in
Felt & Stitch

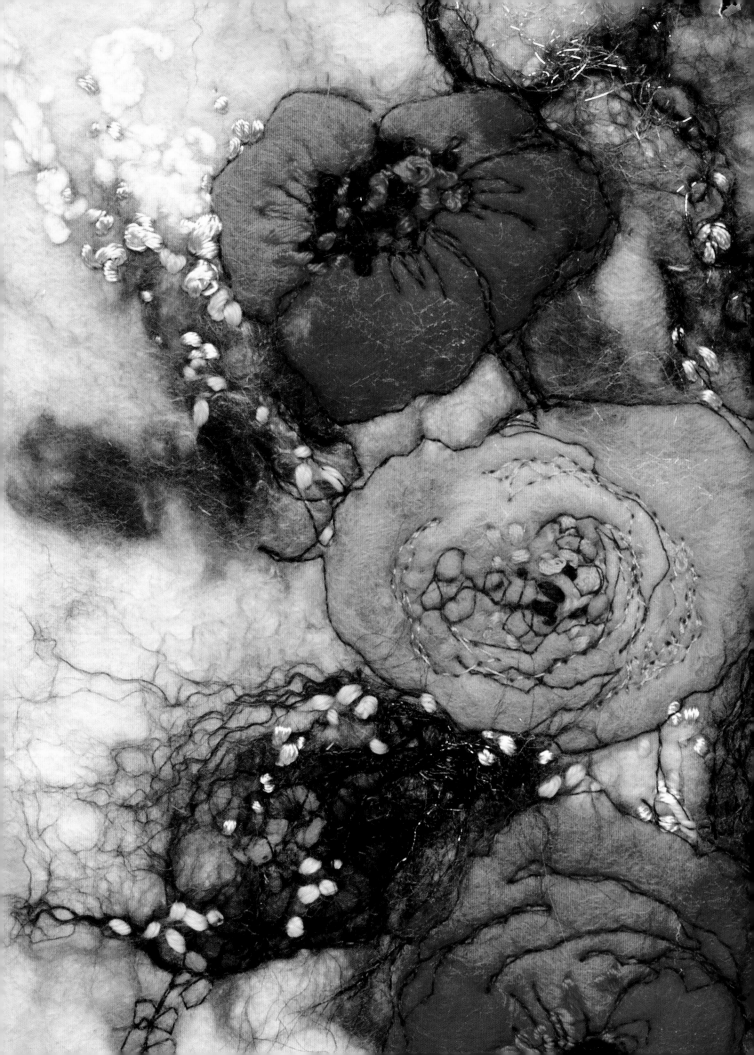

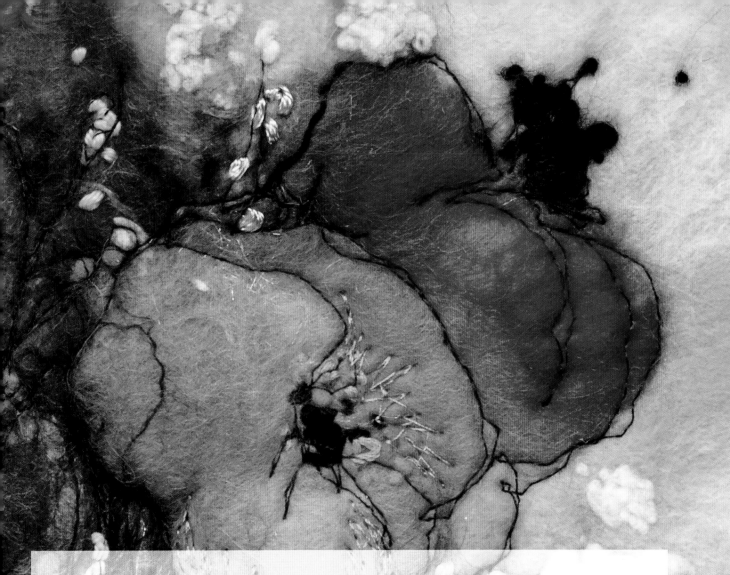

Flowers in
Felt & Stitch

CREATING FLORAL ARTWORKS USING
FLEECE, FIBRES AND THREADS

MOY MACKAY

First published in 2014

Search Press Limited
Wellwood, North Farm Road,
Tunbridge Wells, Kent TN2 3DR

Text copyright © Moy Mackay 2015

Photographs by Paul Bricknell, pages 1, 2–3, 5, 6–7, 8, 9, 12(b), 13, 14, 15, 16, 17, 18, 19, 20–21, 22–23, 24, 25, 26–27, 28, 29, 30, 31, 32, 33, 34, 35, 36, 37, 38–61, 62–85, 86–93, 94, 95, 96, 97, 98, 99, 100, 101, 102–111, 114–115, 118–127, 128 copyright © Search Press Ltd 2014

Additional photographs by Kenneth Martin Photography (front cover flap) and David Cheskin (page 10). All remaining photographs were taken by the author.

Design © Search Press Ltd 2015

ISBN: 978-1-78221-031-3

The Publishers and author can accept no responsibility for any consequences arising from the information, advice or instructions given in this publication.

Readers are permitted to reproduce any of the items/patterns in this book for their personal use, or for the purposes of selling for charity, free of charge and without the prior permission of the Publishers. Any use of the items/patterns for commercial purposes is not permitted without the prior permission of the Publishers. Please ensure that the intellectual property rights of the artist-author are not infringed through commercial exploitation of what you have learned from this book.

For details of suppliers, please visit the Search Press website:
www.searchpress.com

Publisher's note

All the step-by-step photographs in this book feature the author, Moy Mackay. No models have been used.

Printed in China

Dedication

I dedicate this book to my father, Alexander Ramsay Mackay, whose relentless, hard-working genes have helped me through many a late night in my studio.

Acknowledgements

I would like to thank Roz Dace, who was instrumental in introducing me to this artist-author world, which has been a great journey thus far. To Becky Shackleton at Search Press, who endured extra long hours on this book in the studio, and to Deborah Murray for her artistry of words. Finally huge thanks and apologies in equal measure to my partner Johnny and sons Eirinn and Saul, for whom proper home-cooked meals have been a rare occurrence!

Page 1
Blue Thatches at Barley Meadow
40 x 40cm (16 x 16in)
see also pages 114–115.

Pages 2–3
The Spotty Tablecloth (close-up)
30 x 29cm (12 x 11½in)
Including a variety of loosely placed green fibres gives the appearance of soft leaves and foliage without precise detail. The flowerheads are also loose shapes, but are given form and definition through the stitching.

Page 5
Giant Orange Daisies
65 x 26cm (25½ x 10¼in)
see also page 27.

CONTENTS

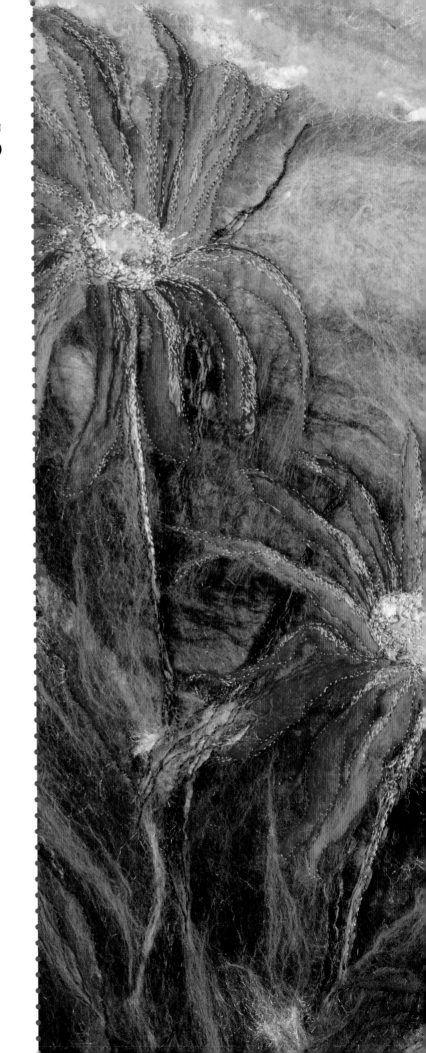

INTRODUCTION

Welcome to my colourful and somewhat fluffy – not to be mistaken with fuzzy – felting world. I cannot imagine a life without art. As soon as I could grasp a crayon I was hooked. Drawing, painting, cutting, gluing and making things are my fondest childhood memories. Colour, in the form of anything art and craft-related, has always been my passion and having been lucky enough to grow up surrounded by various creative family members, I was actively encouraged and hugely inspired from a very young age. I consider myself very lucky – although there has been a lot of hard work and training along the way – to be in a position where I can spend my days doing what I love most. I am eternally grateful to those relatives, friends and teachers who encouraged and supported me along the way. Over the years I have met so many naturally creative people who have been discouraged from embracing this talent, often from their early days at school. In writing this book I hope I can share with you this wonderfully satisfying, therapeutic art form that I have developed over the years. Felt painting is something that can be learned regardless of age, ability or previous art experience.

It was while studying at the wonderful Glasgow School of Art in the late 1980s that I first began to develop my interest in combining painting with textiles. I had always been aware of the perceived differences between fine art and craft, and could not understand why fine art should be seen as more 'worthy'. The wish to bridge this gap fuelled my desire to create a unique art form, one in which I was combining a traditional craft technique with contemporary fine art application. Since those early days, having exhibited at many galleries both at home and abroad, I am happy to say it seems that the gap between 'art' and 'craft' is narrowing. It has been heartening to see my work develop into what is now a recognised art form and one that people genuinely enjoy learning about.

Within these pages I have shared, without exception and in good faith, all the processes I use to create my felted paintings, or 'feltings'. Please find inspiration and guidance at this stage of your felting journey and may this book act simply as a starting point from which you can carry on to develop something unique that you can proudly call your own. Happy felting!

Black Cat with Orange Flowers

38 x 33cm (15 x 13in)

The flat bold black of the cat next to the vibrant, vivid colours and intricate detail of the flowerheads and jug creates an interesting contrast.

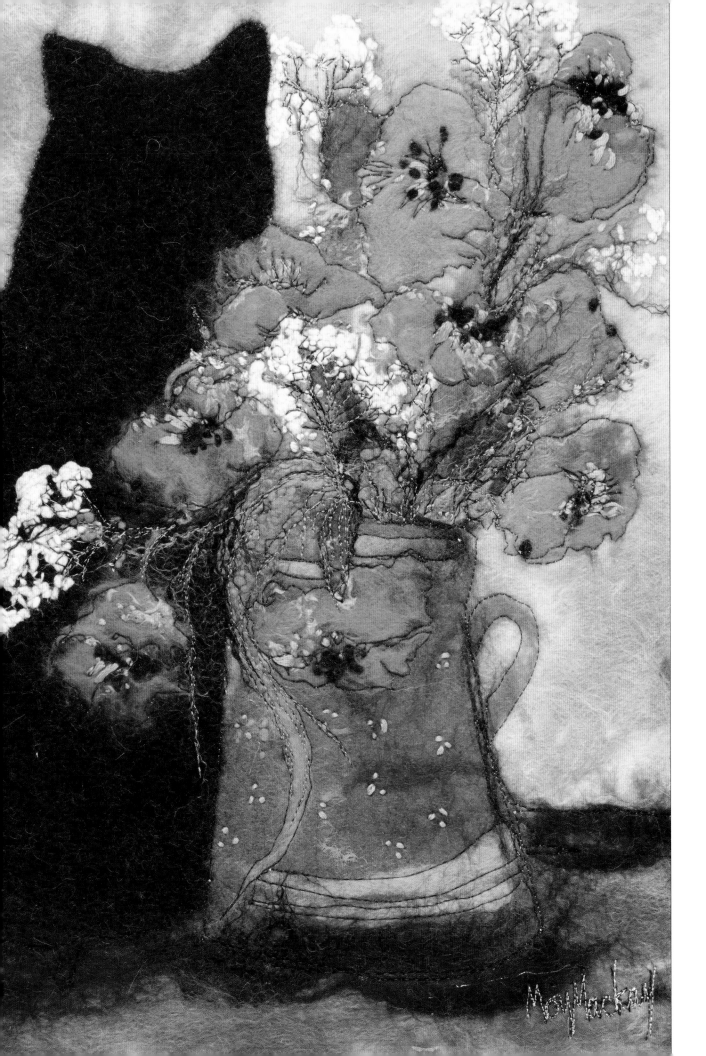

Poppy Croft

35 x 35cm (14 x 14in)

The focus of this piece is the very detailed foreground of poppies. Most of the stitching work is concentrated around the flowers, and the sweeping blues and purples of the sky help to make the flowers really stand out.

Sunflowers

41 x 28cm (16 x 11in)

Shaping the merino into flower and leaf shapes before laying it down gives a good base to work on. Stitched lines are then used to define the shapes further.

MATERIALS AND EQUIPMENT

One of the great things about felt painting is that you don't need vast amounts of equipment or materials to do it, and in fact many of the things you do need will be things you may already have around the house. I find that the best working environment is a sturdy table with a nearby water source and washable floor. In my own studio I use three plastic trestle-style tables, with a drainage pipe positioned in the gaps between the tables to collect the water and direct it into a bucket. This is very effective and cost-efficient. I create my felt paintings on top of bamboo screens, recycled from an old window blind, which allow me to move the feltings around if I need to, and means I can felt them in situ. Add a towel, some plastic garden netting, some soap and hot water and you have all the basic equipment required.

This is a picture of me at work in my studio. I like to surround myself with colourful merino tops as they inspire me, and the other artists around me!

I find the range of merino colours available incredibly inspiring. Remember — if you can't find the exact shade you want you can always blend together other colours to create your own unique palette.

I would advise stocking up on a varied selection of dyed merino tops – although a masterpiece can still be created with a more limited palette if cost is a factor. Merino is available from suppliers worldwide and the colour selection is sublime, from fluorescents to earthier tones, so you may find it difficult to choose just a few! Whatever your choices colour-wise, having a large amount of white merino is advisable: I use this as the base of my feltings as it tends to cost less than dyed tops. I choose to buy my merino tops ready dyed but if you have the time and inclination then dyeing your own can be a rewarding part of the process. I hang up my merino in my studio, as the visual impact is so much greater than if they are buried in a bag or basket. The selection of your colour palette is an important part of the process so it's a good idea to set up some space to hang your lengths of merino if you can.

You will need a set of carders in order to blend and manipulate your fibres. To embellish your felted paintings you will need a basic sewing kit, and a sewing machine on which you can lower the feed dogs and remove the feet, as well as needle felting equipment.

FLEECE

The word 'fleece' generally refers to the wool of a domestic sheep or long-haired goat in its raw state, before it has been washed, treated or dyed. Fleece has been collected and used to make textiles for centuries – some of the oldest known textiles in the world are made from it. Throughout this book I have used the term 'fleece' loosely to describe the wool fibres I use to make my pictures. I mostly work with pre-dyed merino wool tops, see facing page, but feel free to create your felt paintings from raw fleece gathered from the fields or even from your own sheep, if you have them. The characteristics of fleece from different sheep breeds vary greatly and can affect how easily the fibres felt – the ability to felt is dependent mainly upon the length, thickness or quality of the fibre. I have created feltings from all types of fleece. Usually this has been in response to specific sheep-themed commissioned pieces, where farmers have supplied fleece from their prized sheep. These have included Hebridean, Gotland, Lincoln Longwool, Wensleydale and Jacob. All can be used successfully but in my experience, some yield better results and are easier and more pleasurable to work with than others.

12

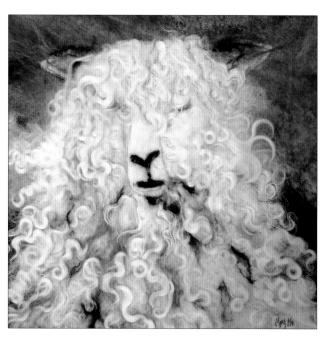

This was a commission in which the customer supplied me with the fleece from her rare breed sheep. The original now hangs in her house while the sheep in question lives on in the garden!

Un-dyed fleece is what we will use to form the base of each picture: the blank canvas onto which we will paint with fibres.

A selection of pre-dyed merino tops. The colour selection is vast and inspiring, from subtle, organic, earthy shades to dazzling pinks and limes.

WOOL TOPS

Wool tops are wool in its semi-processed state: the raw fleece is 'scoured' (washed) then, after drying, it is 'carded' (combed), which teases out and separates the fibres to form a continuous, soft, untwisted rope. Further carding removes the shorter fibres. The remaining long, parallel, well-separated fibres are known as 'tops'. Good-quality tops felt very easily. They are available in various lengths, usually about 5–8cm (2–3in) wide.

Like myself, many felt-makers choose merino tops as their preferred fibre for felting. Merino is very soft, fine wool that is gentle on the hands and, unlike some other natural fibres, is naturally elastic – this is maybe why it seems to me to be the easiest to felt with. It usually originates in either Australia or South America, but is readily available in shops or online. The 's' grade or 'Bradford Count' of the merino denotes the size of the fibre in microns. A micron is a millionth of a metre or $1/25,000$ of an inch and is the way the wool is graded.

The lower the micron the finer the wool. Currently I tend to use mostly 64 s or 70 s quality with a 21-micron count.

What attracted me to merino tops initially was the vast and vibrant selection of coloured fibres available – to me they were the nearest thing in appearance to oil paints. The colours themselves never cease to inspire me, and they adorn a full wall of my studio, where they hang suspended from tall poles like the most colourful, rainbow-like washing line you will ever see. All dyed merino from reputable suppliers should conform to safety standards, which ensure that the fibres are non-toxic, colour-fast and baby-safe. Of course, if you have time you can buy un-dyed merino and colour it yourself – although this is time-consuming it's very rewarding and allows you to create precise shades for your paintings. Merino fibres can be easily blended to create new shades (see pages 42–43), or they can be blended with other fibres to create new and interesting effects.

OTHER FIBRES

Although each felting is mostly composed of merino tops, I like to add in small amounts of other fibres as well. These can be anything from natural or synthetic fibres, hairs and threads, to items such as twigs and glitter – the fun part is experimenting with lots of different 'extras' to see what works. Some will wash away when you wet felt your picture, but don't worry: some bits will stay. If your added extras do wash away, you may find that adding a very fine layer of merino on top next time is enough to keep them in place.

As well as adding in extras, I like to use additional fibres to create specific effects: I like to card silk fibres into merino tops to add a silky sheen to an area of sky, or I might add wool nepps to create the texture of the inside of a flower. Experiment with different fibres to find out how they work and to determine what effects you like. Here are just some of the fibres I use.

Wool nepps.

Wool nepps

Wool nepps are a by-product of the wool industry. They are firm nubs of wool that can be used to add texture and interest to your work – they are good for giving the impression of flowers in a distant field, pebbles on a beach, or for achieving finer details within your flower studies. Take care not to place them too close to each other though, because as the felt shrinks the nepps can clump together – although there may be times when that is exactly the effect you want.

Angelina fibres.

Angelina fibres

Angelina is a unique fibre. It is light reflective, as well as light refractive, which makes it incredibly luminescent. It has a supersoft handle and blended with other fibres in very small amounts it adds sparkle and highlight to your feltings. Angelina comes in three classifications: iridescent, holographic and metallised. My golden rule when using Angelina is that less is definitely more.

Bamboo fibres

Bamboo fibre has many excellent properties that make it ideal for felting: it is exceptionally soft and light and blends well with other fibres; it can also be twisted into very fine strands that can be used to 'draw' with. It has a silky feel, but gives a more matt finish than silk fibres.

Merino rovings

Rovings are merino tops that have been drawn out into pencil-thin, continuous strands prior to twisting. They can be used to add bulk to your felting.

Soya bean fibre

This 100 per cent protein fibre is made from soya beans and is suitable for vegans who may prefer not to use silk. It is very soft, smooth and light with a delicate shine and has a natural creamy yellow colour, similar to tussah silk.

Bamboo fibres.

Other animal fibres

Many other animal fibres can also be used for felting, including alpaca, camel, yak and goat. Dog and cat hair will also felt well when blended with merino, and could form the basis of a very special, personalised painting.

SILKS

Subtle textures can be achieved by blending different coloured silks into your merino during carding, while smaller amounts or strands can be added on top to add finer definition and detail. These silky smooth fibres are lovely to handle and will add a beautiful sheen to your work.

Mulberry silk

This is a soft and lustrous fibre and is good for creating fine outlines – the fibres tend to sit on top of the merino, without becoming too felted, which can work wonderfully. It is available in a gorgeous range of colours.

White silk noil

Superb quality white silk fibres that can be carded with merino for added texture. This silk fibre contains noil fragments remaining from the silk cocoon.

Tussah silk noil

Tussah silk fibres are available as a pale cream carded mass of fibres and have a silky handle. A small amount of silk noil carded in fleece produces a lovely textured effect.

Tussah silk sliver

This is a lustruous, high-quality fibre. In its un-dyed form it has a pale golden, honey-like colour.

Italian silk waste

These fibres are soft, de-gummed and curly; this high gloss fibre is the textured version of silk tops.

Silk fibres.

Wet felting equipment

Carders

Available from good felt-making suppliers, carders are pads or boards covered with hooked wire bristles; they often have handles made of wood and come as a pair. Fibres are brushed between two carders in order to prepare or blend them (see pages 39–41).

Soap

Any type of soap will do! I generally use soap flakes, but olive oil soap and diluted mild shampoo are also popular options. You can even use diluted washing-up liquid, but it may prove hard on your hands.

Garden netting

I like to use fine plastic garden netting, which is available from garden centres or online, to protect the surface of my paintings during wet felting – it allows me to agitate and felt the fibres without disturbing or moving the elements of the painting around too much.

Non-dyed muslin and bubblewrap can also be used for this purpose, but although they are easier on the hands, I find that muslin can sometimes attach itself to the fibres of your painting during felting, while bubblewrap can slide around, giving you less control over your work.

Bamboo blinds

I like to work directly on large bamboo blinds, layering the fibres on top: this allows me to move the piece easily and safely before felting if I need to, and means that the felt picture is ready in situ when I come to felt. Bamboo blinds can be bought fairly inexpensively in hardware shops, and can often be found in second hand or charity shops. Remove any metal fittings before use. For smaller pieces of work, bamboo place mats or sushi mats work well – remove any excess dye from them first. Rubberised sticky mats are also a handy addition as they will stop the bamboo mat from sliding about as you roll.

Hand carders are great for blending together different colours and fibres, especially if you want a thorough blend. Dog brushes are a handy alternative if you can't get hold of the real thing. If you want to blend large amounts of fibres then consider investing in a drum carding machine.

Ridged felting tools

Made of hardwood, a ridged rolling pin – which is used just like a regular rolling pin – is designed to make working and finishing your felt easy. It is used to exert pressure on the fibres during the felting process, usually after they have been rubbed by hand. You can also use the roller after you've rinsed your painting, when the felt is still damp, to even up any soft spots or to make the piece harder all over. Alternatively, there are other ridged tools available, in various shapes and sizes, which are great for massaging into the surface of your painting to encourage the fibres to bind together.

Other equipment

A measuring jug is useful for pouring hot water over the felt during the felting process and a washing-up bowl or bucket is handy to collect any excess water if you don't have a sink in your workspace.

Old towels or chamois can make the rolling process easier. If you wrap a towel or chamois around your bundle before rolling it, it will prevent it from slipping about too much. This is particularly useful if you are working on a slippery table top or hard floor surface. Alternatively, they can be laid flat on the table or surface that you are rolling on to absorb water and prevent slippage. They will also come in very handy for mopping up excess soap and water at the end.

If, like myself, you are allergic to some soap products, or have sensitive skin in general, I would suggest wearing rubber gloves during the wet felting process. They will also make handling very hot and very cold water more bearable.

Lengths of wooden dowling, a broom handle or expanded foam swimming 'noodles' can be used during the rolling stage of wet felting, but aren't essential. Place at the edge of your wet fleece then roll it up with the broom handle in the middle. The presence of the handle will apply extra pressure on the felt and help the process to occur with a bit less physical effort – this can be especially handy when working on very large pieces of felt.

These are the regular items I use in my work – use the advice given here to choose the tools that are right for you.

Needle felting equipment

Felting needles

These are extremely sharp, with tiny notches, or barbs, cut near the tip of the shaft, so take great care when working with them. The notches are cut at an upward angle so that as the needles are repeatedly poked into the felt the fibres catch in the notches and become entangled. The technique is ideal for adding embellishment, creating areas of shading or repositioning elements that have moved during the felting process.

The size of the felting needle is indicated by its gauge. The higher the gauge the finer and more delicate the needle. Different gauged needles have different effects on the wool, but I find finer needles best suited for embellishing felt paintings: I tend to use 38 and 40 gauge needles. The needles are available in different shapes – triangular and star-shaped. It is worth buying a selection of sizes and shapes to experiment with, and buy a few extra as they tend to break easily! Multi-needled tools are also available, and are good for working on large areas, but I find that using a single needle gives more control for creating fine detail.

Foam

When needle felting it is essential that you place a piece of dense foam beneath your work – it should be at least 5cm (2in) thick, but the thicker the better. Ideally it should be about the same size as your painting, but you could use a smaller piece of foam and move your work around on top of it. The needle will poke into the foam as it pierces the felt; without it the needle will break and your work surface will be damaged.

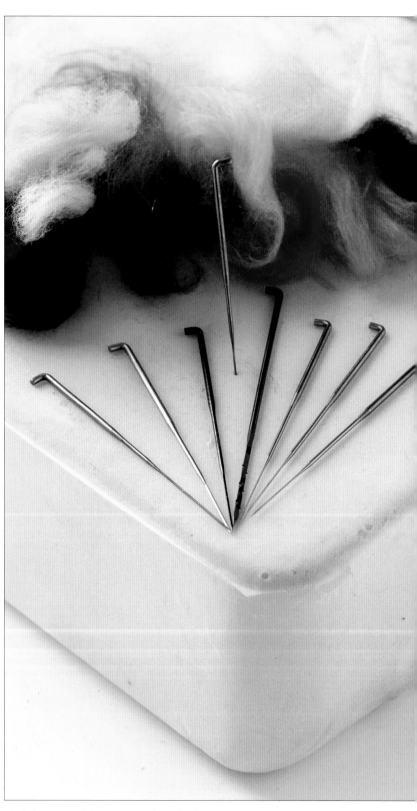

The thicker the foam the better as it provides good cushioning for your needles. This dense piece of foam was taken from an orthopedic chair, and is the ideal thickness.

STITCHING EQUIPMENT

Sewing machine

To sew in a loose, freehand manner, you will need a machine that you can set to a straight stitch, remove the foot and lower the feed dog. Some machines are capable of doing decorative stitches, which can also look good incorporated into your work. It's a good idea to experiment with various types and sizes of needles. You may need to experiment with different needle weights depending on the thickness of your felting.

Machine threads

As well as regular poly-cotton threads, I like to use silk types when I want a glossier line. They come in a huge selection of colours as well as rainbow mixes, which can give an interesting effect. Choose a range of threads that will complement your merino palette and be sure to have some black and white, too. Don't be afraid to experiment – try using different weights and types of threads, as all may give a different, interesting end result.

Hand embroidery threads

Try to accumulate a range of colours and thicknesses to use in your hand embroidery. You can use any type of thread, from cotton, metallic and chunky six-stranded embroidery silk to wool, string and even thin wire.

Embroidery needles

Most embroidery needles should work well with your felting, but try to avoid those with very large eyes, as this may result in visible holes in the felt. I personally find sharper needles easier to work with.

Snippers and scissors

Be sure to have a pair of sharp scissors to work with. During the embellishing and embroidery stages I find that snippers are best, as they allow me to trim threads neatly and more closely to the felt than scissors do.

Iron-on backing

Before starting to embroider it is a good idea to attach some sort of backing to your felt. This can be iron-on interfacing or something similar. It will help to protect your sewing machine from felt dust as well as stiffening the work before further embellishment.

Iron

Essential for attaching iron-on backing. If you happen to have a crease or unwanted lumps in your work after felting then an iron can help to flatten these out.

Treat yourself to a good selection of coloured threads to complement the merino shades you have used; a variety of thicknesses and textures will add an extra dimension to your work.

INSPIRATION

Inspiration can come from many places: stormy skies, the grass beneath your feet or the flowers in your garden. By studying even the smallest daisy you have the basis for a wonderful felted creation. I cannot stress highly enough the importance of really looking at what's around you, and taking the time to observe fine detail, such as the colours, forms and patterns, so that you carry these details through into your work and bring it to life.

Whether you are planning a still life or a landscape, a good starting point is to study real flowers around you. Cut flowers in a vase, growing in a windowbox or in the garden all make good subjects. With a camera or smartphone it is easy to capture anything that inspires you when you are out and about, but if you prefer to eschew technology, a sketchbook is also good for documenting ideas that you may want to incorporate into your felt paintings at a later stage.

But don't limit yourself – inspiration can come from all kinds of sources. It could be an image you see in a magazine or on a card, a colour combination you particularly like, or a work by your favourite artist – take inspiration from all sorts of sources. The most important part of your creative journey is to develop these ideas and inspirations into something that is truly and uniquely yours. This will give your work life and freshness. The sense of achievement when we know we have created something we can call our own is second to none.

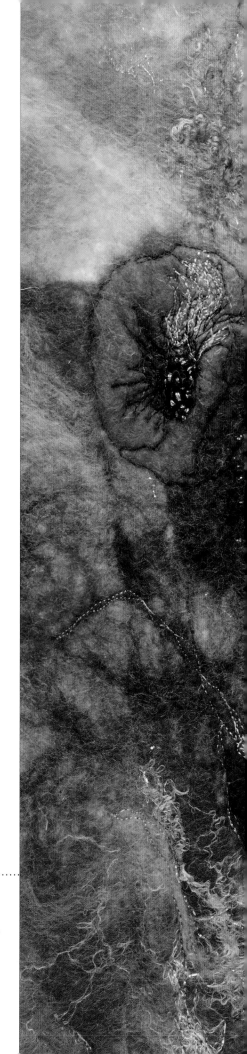

Margaret and John's Mecanopsis

37 x 37cm (14½ x 14½in)

In this piece I created the background as I would a landscape, then worked only on the poppies, leaving the background undefined and quite hazy. I used Angelina fibres and gold embroidery thread to give the piece some extra sparkle.

DEVELOPING YOUR IDEAS

The first thing I do when contemplating a new piece of work is to consider the set-up. If a piece is to be a still life composition I will consider the type of flower, the vase that will hold it, where it's going to be positioned and so on. Without doubt, the best paintings are achieved when you have the real objects in front of you. Try out different elements of your composition: consider the height of the flower compared with the height or width of your vase or container; choose coloured or patterned containers that will contrast well with your flower colours and shapes, or use a treasured or cherished item; and choose a background texture – whether that be plain wood, for example, or a striped or checked tablecloth. The main considerations for me are colour combinations, proportion and background. It's good to play around at this stage, step back and see the elements in an unfocused way, particularly if you tend to worry about detail too much. All these elements can contribute a different feel or mood to your piece, so play around until you are happy. In preparation for a piece I find it helpful to do detailed exercises such as sketches and paintings, and sometimes I will create a moodboard for a piece, containing elements such as fibre samples, pressed flowers, mixed media drawings and photographs.

Capturing detail

Use media such as pens and pencils to focus on the detail of a subject – any subtleties you capture at this stage can be later transposed into your felting. I also find it helpful to do pencil sketches when I am paying particular attention to areas of light and shade. Roughly block in areas of tone, then step back and look at your sketches in an unfocused way, as mentioned above.

Capturing colour

Use paints, pastels and torn paper collages to practise creating the subtle colour variations of your chosen subject – experimenting with them at this stage can help to inform your felt choices later on. Keep fibre samples to hand – experiment with blending different colours and fibre types so that you can create the precise shades and effects you need.

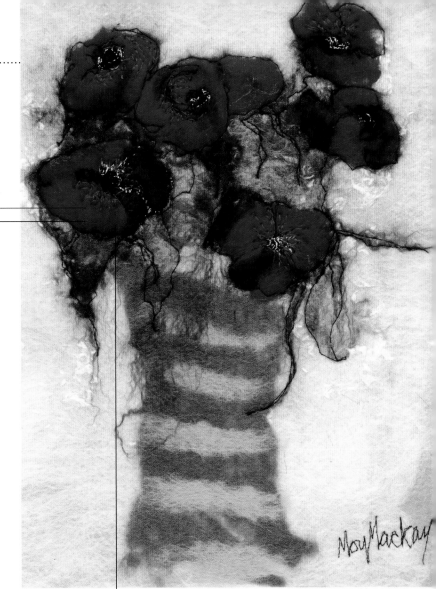

The Stripy Vase

26 x 23cm (10¼ x 9in)

Before creating this piece I did pen drawings of the poppies to help familiarise myself with their form and detail. These were particularly useful when embellishing and allowed me to create my own interpretation while still remaining faithful to the original. I also did some pastel drawings and glued various fibres to them to give an idea of what might work well at the felt painting stage. As I had no access to real poppies I studied various photographs of poppies and compiled a moodboard to gather all this information together.

Sketches

Helpful for studying a subject's form, sketches should be done from a range of different angles. You'll connect with some more than others, which will help you to narrow down your final arrangement.

Photographs

Collecting together photographs of your chosen subject can help to inform you later on – it is especially helpful to have a range of images to refer to if you are creating a landscape or working on a subject that you don't have in front of you.

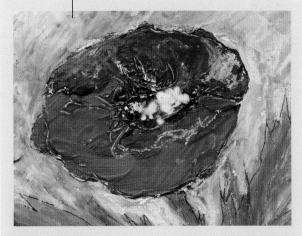

Paintings

Creating sketchy paintings of your subject can help you to familiarise yourself with the colours and tones you'll be working with. Mix up different media to create a more expressive, dynamic piece of work.

Moodboards

Creating moodboards can be a fun way of gathering all your ideas and visual inspirations in one place. You can add photographs, drawings, collages, colour swatches, merino and thread samples, dried flowers or sweet wrappers – anything and everything that excites and inspires you. Having these around you when you work can really help, and it's also a fun exercise to get those creative juices flowing. One such moodboard I created prior to a felting included a torn paper collage. This is useful if you do not yet feel confident sketching or painting. I like to give various textures and weights of paper quick washes of paint so that I have a variety to choose from. It is a great way to get a feel for an object as you are following its shape and form while carefully tearing the papers. Drawing on top of these with pen can also be a good way of depicting areas you may want to enhance later with machine stitch.

Here are a few more ideas for items that you might want to add to your moodboard. Pressed flowers and leaves can also be good for reference – it's worth taking the time to dry and prepare them in order to preserve as much of their original detail as possible. Mixed media drawings are a great start to any felting and well worth a try. I like to combine paint, oil pastel and pen. Developing moodboards in this way can help to eradicate any fears you may have of embarking on a new project. You will have already made your key decisions and choices before you even pick up your fibres, so you can relax and enjoy your felting experience!

Painting on location

Due to the weather in Scotland it is, sadly, not possible to work on a felt painting outside. The first gust of wind would see the fibres fly off into the ether. If you are in the same situation, the next best thing is to go out with a small sketchbook to do some quick drawings or paintings documenting a composition you may like to develop further. It is not essential to add fine details, rather to give an idea of placement and colour.

Painting from photographs

Another good exercise is to create paintings and sketches based on photographs you've taken. This will help you become more observant of composition and can help you to narrow down what aspects of the photograph you want to include in the final piece.

The Red-roofed Bothy

23 x 21cm (9 x 8¼in)

This simple composition featuring a bothy, or mountain shelter, is transformed into an elaborate garden thanks to an abundance of coloured stitches. Working directly from a couple of preliminary paintings, I chose to keep some aspects and deviate from others, using the parts I liked best from each. Adapting original drawings or ideas is a healthy part of the process. It can also increase your confidence in judging the progress of your felt painting and enable you to make changes as and when necessary.

Pen drawings

These are particularly good for depicting fine details. When I reach the machine embroidery stage it is the fine lines from pen studies that I try to re-create.

Mixed media drawings

Pastels are staples of mine when sketching. I feel they achieve the closest resemblance to the appearance of a felted painting. By using them in the initial stages you will get a good sense of how your finished piece could look. I often use the pastels loosely and then will add the finer detail and fine lines and marks by using pen on top.

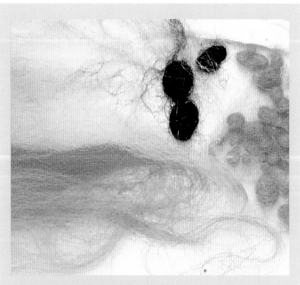

Torn paper collages

I find that creating flower shapes from torn paper is a very freeing exercise: you cannot be as precise as with other media, and you may well find that you unintentionally create pleasing shapes that you later decide to transfer to your felting composition.

Felt and fibre samples

Collect different colours and fibres and practise blending together small amounts to see what effects you can achieve.

Pressed flowers

Preserved for reference, pressed or dried flowers can be a useful resource when creating a composition – save any favourite or special flowers, in case they are out of season when you come to create your felting.

Giant Orange Daisies

65 x 26cm (25½ x 10¼in)

Working from my fine pen drawings was a good starting point for this piece. During the process I decided I would rather see the daisies rugged and windswept, as the background I had chosen was more of a landscape setting. My initial exercises made it easier to adapt the daisies into different positions.

COLOUR

I love the ways in which colour can inspire and excite. The thrill I get when I see the contrast of bright sunshine against a gunmetal sky, or the sparkle of flowers after rain is both uplifting and energising. I believe in the power of colour therapy and am heartened that some forward-thinking schools and hospitals are recognising the effect colour has on our actions, moods and well-being, and choosing their décor accordingly. The same applies to the works you create. Think about the mood you wish to present: if you are looking to create a botanical study then keep it on white or a light, non-obtrusive background so that all the focus is directed at the detail in your work. Bold, bright colours will give the work more of a fun, contemporary and uplifting feel, whereas more subdued hues will come across as more mellow.

Daffodils and Narcissi

33 x 33cm (13 x 13in)

Consider the background colour before starting a flower composition. It helps to have an opposing colour if you want the flowers to stand out.

Poppies with Fiona's Belties

28 x 28cm (11 x 11in)

Here I want to show how, by using flat bold sections of colour, we end up with a more abstract and less realistic piece. Experimenting with flat colour in a very free form makes for some interesting results.

The vivid colour palette of merino was what actually started my exploration of the art of felting. I love to paint, especially with oil paints, as there is such a rich range of colours available, but I don't love the length of time it takes for them to dry! With this in mind I sought to find a medium that would give the same vibrancy and depth, yet in a more immediate way. To this day I am still intrigued by the endless possibilities of what can be created by blending different fibres together. You can use different combinations of merino fibres to create tone, light and shadow within your work, use complementary colours to striking effect, or even use flat expanses of colour and then create detail using stitching. It's important to take the time to really observe your flower subjects before you select your fibres, and also to decide on the style of your piece: for some, such as the flowers shown left, you may want to use a range of coloured fibres, such as red, pink and orange, within each bloom. Alternatively, you may want to create very simple, one-tone petals, see above, and then add in the detail when you stitch.

If you are not confident when using colour, do some preparatory moodboards. Collect colours that you like in any form, be it scraps of paper, paint charts, wrappers, fabric swatches, feathers or leaves. Play around with the position of the colours until you find a colour combination you like. I would suggest you explore all sorts of colour combinations, even the ones you don't particularly gravitate to. You may discover that some, even those that you thought might not work, create unexpectedly beautiful effects. My main advice when working with colour is to enjoy it, play with it and most importantly – do not be frightened by it.

Heart-shaped Biscuit

29 x 29cm (11½ x 11½in)

By choosing interesting colour and tone combinations, you give the flowers an extra depth they wouldn't have if simply made from one flat colour.

Oranges and Lemons

35 x 28cm (14 x 11in)

Despite being a simple composition, the vibrancy of the yellows against the purples, pinks and greens makes this piece really striking.

Summer Meadow

45 x 28cm (18 x 11in)

This is a very simple landscape composition, but by the addition of a rainbow of coloured threads and embroidery stitches, a vibrant, gorgeous summer meadow is formed.

Flowers from Johnny, Christmas 2013

37 x 21cm (14½ x 8in)

This piece has a relatively simple palette of colours: I chose to complement the pink of the roses and lilies and the green of their foliage with a soft purple and lilac background. For this still life piece I worked directly from a bouquet of lilies, roses and greenery, picking out just some of the leaves in detail, leaving others as soft, painterly shapes.

ADDING TEXTURE AND DETAIL

There are several processes involved in creating my feltings. Firstly the 'painting' stage, which is wet felted. Then comes the needle felting, followed by freehand machine embroidery and finally the piece is finished with hand stitching. In each of these stages, but especially the last three, the aim is to add fine detail and texture to a piece.

Not everyone who embarks on a felted painting will want to do the stitching. It is therefore good practice to add finer detail during the first 'painting' stage. Within the projects in this book you will learn how to achieve fine details by the careful placement of fibres, silks and threads. You can then incorporate these into your work as you would when using pen, or a fine brush in a painting. In addition to my merino staple I have an ever-growing collection of all sorts of weird and wonderful natural and synthetic fibres that I like to experiment with when adding a further dimension to my work.

Many felt-makers are taught never to use scissors when working with merino. For me, the use of scissors is an integral part of my process. It can achieve sharp and definite angles and can be a means of getting tiny fibres into chosen sections of work.

The Little Brown Jug

23 x 23cm (9 x 9in)

The stitched detail in this piece helps bring it to life: outlining the flowers in black machine thread highlights their delicate shapes and adds interest and texture to the piece, while the thick embroidery threads used give a shiny texture and an extra injection of colour. Using a dark background makes the vibrant flowers really pop out.

After a piece of work has been wet felted I will needle felt it. Using a barbed felting needle along with a very small amount of merino fibres, I will re-work any aspects of the piece I feel would benefit from further shading or additional detail. It is an effective means of adding tiny details like doors and windows or linear patterns to a flower or stem.

Next comes freehand machine embroidery: I use this to outline and add detail to my feltings. It is worth having a range of colours and thread types to choose from, as you can create some wonderful effects. The final embellishment I like to add is hand stitching. Using a variety of thread textures and stitch types will enhance the work further. I choose to add very little in the way of embellishment to some pieces of my work, while with others it's hard to know when a piece is 'finished'. With practice you will learn to recognise which pieces of work will benefit most from further working and which don't need it. The secret is knowing when to stop!

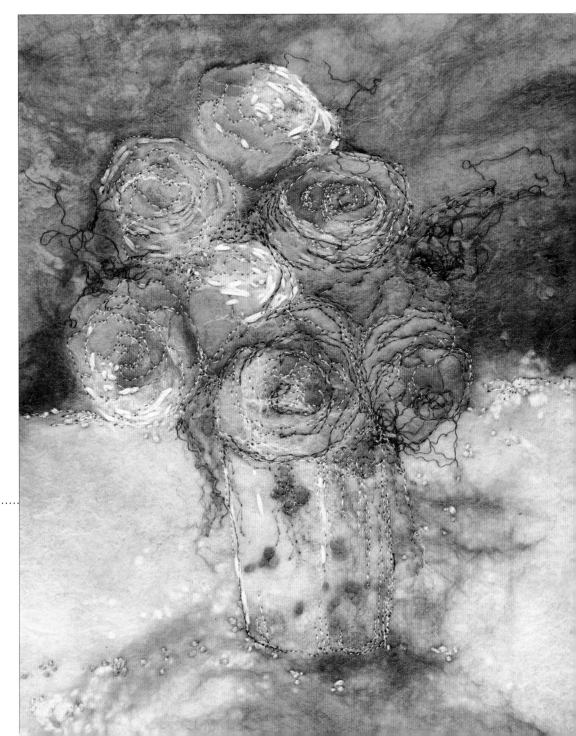

....
Ranunculus

31 x 26cm (12¹⁄₄ x 10¹⁄₄in)
You can create really interesting effects by using lots of wiggling lines of machine stitching to outline intricate flower shapes. To portray the delicate, paper-like quality of this flower I kept the fibres thin to give an almost translucent quality.

Summer Mix

38 x 27cm (15 x 10¾in)

*By combining threads and silks in
the felting process, interesting lines
and shapes have formed that give
fine detail within the foliage.*

Teacake and Flowers

32 x 28cm (13 x 11in)

*It is interesting to use unfamiliar
items in still life compositions,
especially when their shapes and
textures contrast with your flowers.
Here, I have chosen an iconic
cottish delicacy with its distinctive
shiny wrapper.*

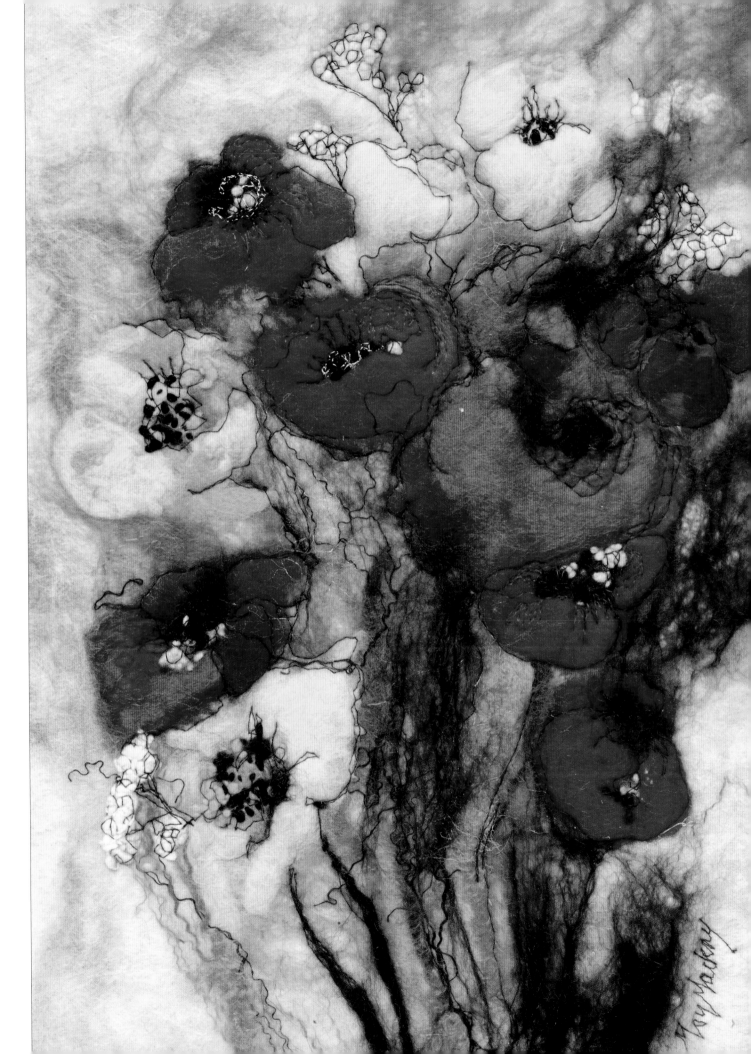

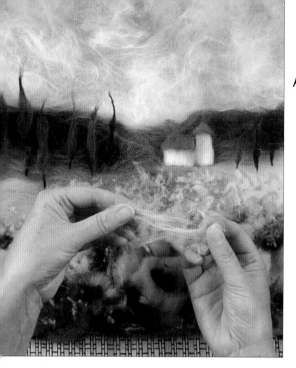

TECHNIQUES

This section covers all the techniques you need to know to create beautiful feltings of your own. We will take one project and follow it from beginning to end, covering the whole process in detail. To begin with, I will demonstrate how to blend together merino fibres to create your own colour palette – a process known as carding. From here you will learn to create a felt base for your pictures, and then I will guide you through laying down your colours and mixing up your fibres in order to create your picture. The actual felting process itself, which uses nothing more than soap and hot water, is explained in easy-to-follow steps. Finally I will show you how you can define and embellish your felt painting using needle felting, and machine and hand stitching. The techniques are easy to learn and require just a few basic skills and a bit of imagination.

Before you start, consider how long the processes will take: allow a few hours for composing your felt masterpiece, then a further one or two for the felting process. You will need to allow your felting to dry completely before you work on it further – the embellishment stage itself can take as much or as little time as you want. To make life easy for yourself, create your picture on the same surface that you will eventually felt it on, to prevent having to move it – a large kitchen table covered with towels to absorb excess felting water can be ideal.

CARDING

The process of carding involves combing fibres together using a pair of carders – paddles covered with tiny, curved hooks – although dog brushes or even your fingers will do the same job on small amounts of fleece. Use the carders to blend two or more colours together to create a new colour. The longer you card for, the more evenly blended the colours will be. For a mottled effect, stop before the colours are fully blended; this will allow you to create a variety of colour and tone within your work. To create interesting textures, card the merino with other fibres such as bamboo or silk.

I Lay a little of each coloured fleece on one of the carders, so that the fibres lie in the same direction as the handle. Use about 1cm (½in) thick pieces – too little merino is difficult to card while too much will just fall off.

2 Place the second carder on top, with the handle facing in the opposite direction – the hooks on each will be pointing in different directions. Pull the carders away from each other, combing the fleece as you do so.

3 Pull the two carders apart – the fleece will now be trapped between the needles, some on the top carder and some on the bottom.

4 Continue to comb the fleece between the carders for a few more minutes. To ensure that the colours start to blend, move the top carder higher or lower relative to the bottom one, ensuring that the dark blue of one is combed against the light blue of the other.

5 To release the fibres, turn the carders so that the handles are both facing down. Position the top of the right hand carder against the bottom of the left hand carder. Push the right hand carder upwards, across the left hand carder, causing the fibres to peel away.

Tip

Transferring the fibres at this stage will make carding much quicker – the light blue of the right hand carder will now be directly on top of the dark blue of the left hand carder, and vice versa.

6 The fleece is now transferred to the left hand carder – the fibres may still be quite unmixed at this stage.

7 Continue to comb the fibres together, repeating steps 2–4 to get a good blend of colour.

8 Remove the fibres from the top carder again, using the same technique as in step 5.

9 For additional colour and texture, add in some mid-blue bamboo fibres. Tease them out and spread them thinly on top of the carded fibres.

10 Blend in the bamboo fibres by combing the fibres together, repeating steps 2–4.

11 Add in some silk noil fibres for extra colour and texture. Lay them on top of the carded fibres then blend them in using steps 2–4. When you are happy with the blend of your fibres, remove them from your carders using the technique given in step 5.

The carded fleece, with bamboo fibres and silk noil mixed in.

CARDED COLOURS

The table below shows a variety of merino colour combinations, the colours they produce when carded and what they look like once felted. Remember, the longer you card for, the more the fibres will be mixed and the more blended the end result. Carding for a short time will produce a more mottled effect, which you may prefer.

Uncarded merino fibres

Carded fibres

Felted fibres

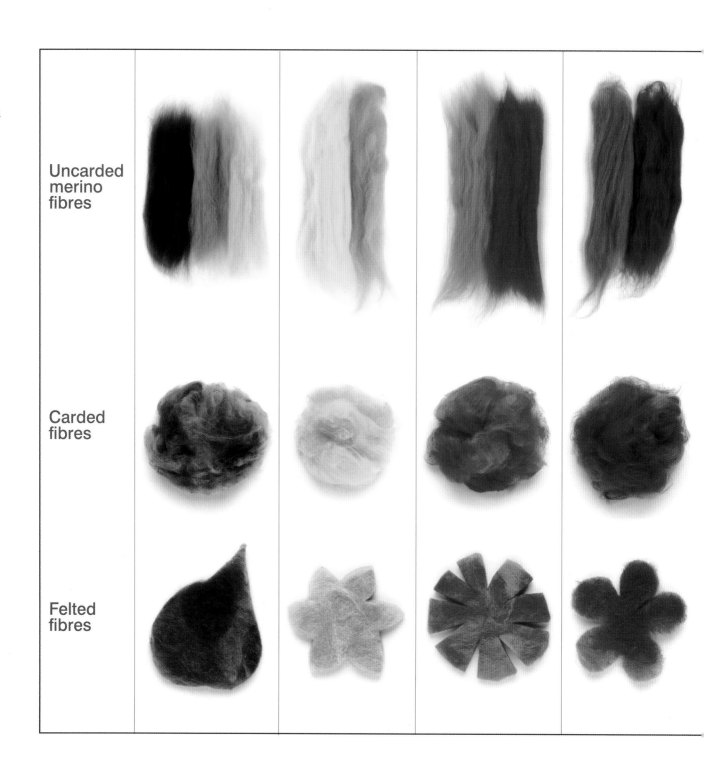

Carding results

The fleece on the right has been carded for longer, resulting in a more uniform colour. Experiment with colours, fibres and carding times, as the more variety you create, the more interesting your feltings will be.

LAYERING THE FIBRES

Prepare your work surface: if you need to, lay down a towel or two first, to absorb the excess water from the felting process, then roll out your bamboo mat on top.

You will start by creating a thick, even layer of merino wool – white is a good choice as it is often cheaper than coloured types and will show off the other colours to their full advantage, but you could use any colour you want. For a picture approximately 30cm (12in) square, allow about 1m (39in) of merino.

When creating your base, work with a loose, soft touch – often the fibres will not separate easily unless handled gently. Layer up your fibres thinly and slowly, as though you were painting with watercolour – thick, uneven clumps may not matt together well and might make your picture look lumpy.

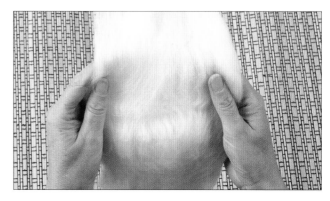

1 To create your base you will need about 1m (39in) of merino, divided into four equal pieces. Gently tease it apart – if you pull it gently the fibres will separate easily. Space your hands about 20cm (8in) apart as you do so.

2 Unravel each piece, teasing the fibres out until each measures about 15cm (6in) wide and 1cm (½in) deep, with no holes or gaps.

3 Lay your pieces of merino on your bamboo mat with the fibres running vertically. Position the pieces so that they are touching and aligned top and bottom, then tease out and overlap the fibres where they meet to create a neat, even join. Don't worry too much about keeping the outer edges of the square neat.

4 Lay the third piece of merino, with its fibres lying horizontally, across the top of your square – make sure its edges line up with the pieces below. Finally, lay the fourth piece below, teasing out and overlapping the fibres at the join to create a thick, even, square base.

5 Have a look through your fibres and work out what your colour and fibre palette will be: here, the background is covered with the carded blue merino made on pages 39–41 and a carded yellow and orange; the vase is teal; carded reds and greens are used for the flowers, with highlights and shadows created throughout. Also pick out any additional fibres – here, white wool nepps, green, red and blue bamboo fibres and red and green Angelina have been used.

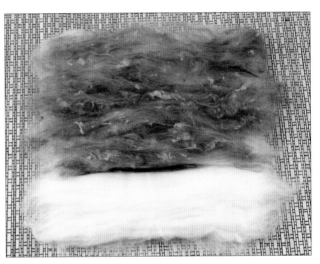

6 It's always best to create the background first and to work from the top downwards. Take your carded blue fleece and tease the fibres so that they all run in the same direction. Lay it down across the top of the picture.

7 Cover about two-thirds of the piece with the carded blue fibres, making sure that you achieve an even coverage. It doesn't matter if some of the white shows through – the density of the fibres is up to you.

8 Card together some yellow and orange merino fibres, following the instructions on pages 39–41. Tease the fibres out so that they all lie in the same direction, then place an even layer over the bottom third of the picture.

Tip
A good technique when laying down fine horizontal strips is to place them down on the left, hold them in place, then tease the fibres across to the right.

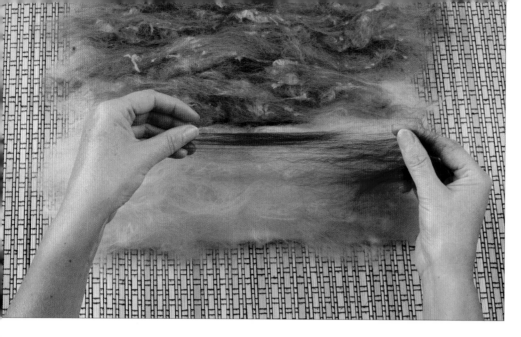

9 To create areas of shading, take some uncarded brown merino and tease it out until it is quite fine. Lay a thin line of this along the join between the blue and yellow fibres, and place a few larger pieces down the right hand side.

Tip

Keep the dark brown fibres fine so that the orange-yellow background shows through.

10 Tease out some thin wisps of black merino, and place these on the bottom right of the blue, with a few small pieces up the right hand side.

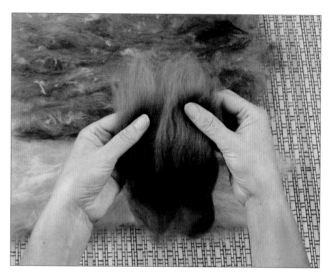

11 To create the vase, spread out a piece of uncarded teal merino, taking care not to make any holes or gaps between the fibres as you do so.

12 Use a pair of sharp fabric scissors to cut out an oval vase shape from the merino.

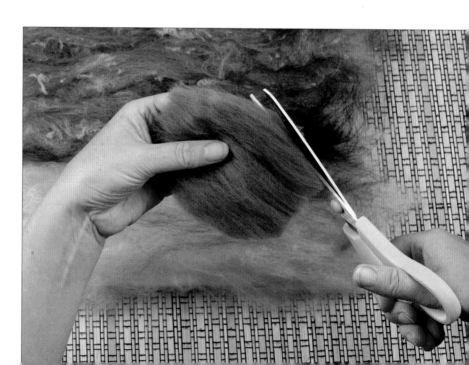

13 To give the vase a rounded appearance, tease out some pale blue fibres and arrange them on the left hand side of your vase; as you work, keep in mind that your imagined light source is coming from the left. Take the vase off the picture and set aside carefully.

14 Tease out a number of strands of dark and light green carded merino and twist the ends to create leaf-like shapes. Arrange them on the background as shown, overlapping them and bending them forward to give the impression of a mass of leaves.

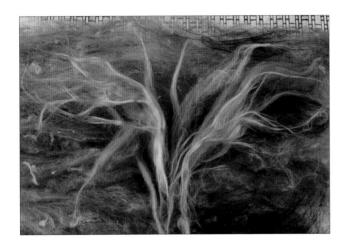

15 Tease out some slightly shorter lengths of light green bamboo fibre, twist the ends loosely, and lay these on top to create another set of leaves.

Tip

Remember that fibres such as bamboo and silk won't matt into the felt in the same way as merino fibres – instead they will remain as distinct fibres on top of the felted fabric.

16 Position the vase on your picture, covering the bottoms of your stems and making sure that they all fit behind it, then bend some of the leaves forward over the top.

Tip

The beauty of felt painting is that you can play around with the fibres. Place them on, move them around, take them off. You will soon learn what works to get the effect you want.

17 Card together some light and dark red merino fibres, following the instructions on pages 39–41. Shape a small amount of it into a ball, tucking in the ends and making a slight indentation in the centre.

18 Position the flowerhead on top of one of the stems, then create and position a second.

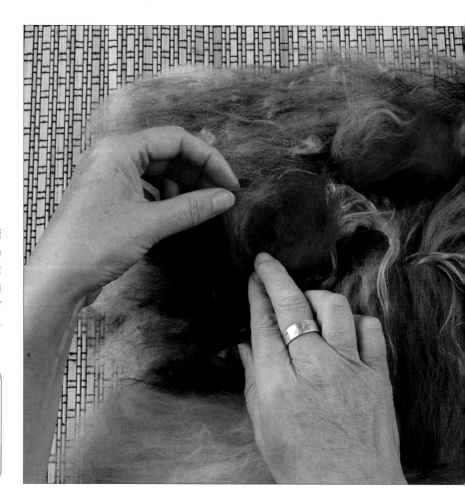

19 Tease out a few strands of uncarded orange merino and position them on the upper left side of your flowers, remembering that this is the side closest to your imaginary light source.

Tip

Adding colourful highlights to your picture helps to bring it to life – when felted, it will appear as though light is bouncing off the petals.

20 Think of this part of the composition like flower arranging, and add in a few more flowers, following steps 17 and 18. Play around with the arrangement until you are happy with it.

21 Using uncarded black merino, add some dark tones to your picture: arrange some fine strands around the bottom and right hand sides of each flower and on the right hand side of the vase. Twist the ends of some thin strands, so that they are neat and pointed, and nestle a few among the leaves.

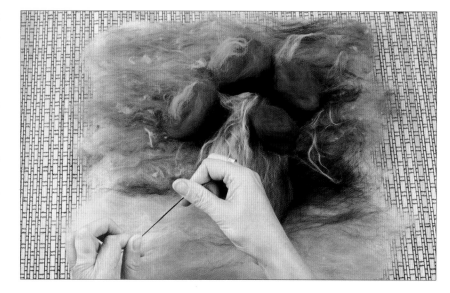

22 Create three small balls of black merino, tucking the ends in to get them as rounded as possible.

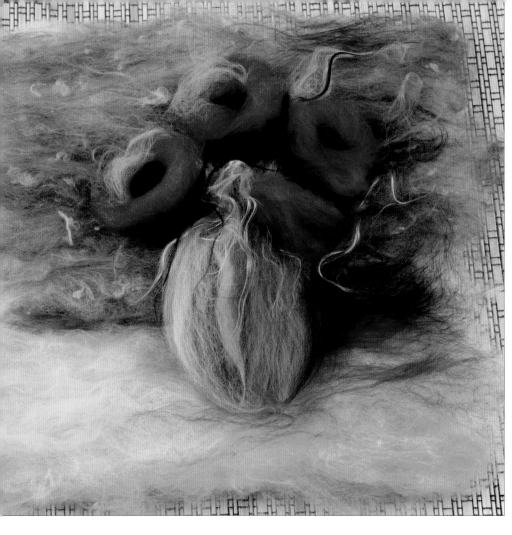

23 Position a black merino ball in the centre of each of the top three flowers, tucking the balls into the indentations so that they are secure and partly hidden.

24 With the main elements complete it's time to add on the finishing touches. Position a few white wool nepps in the centre of the top three flowers; they should sit on the edge of the black centres.

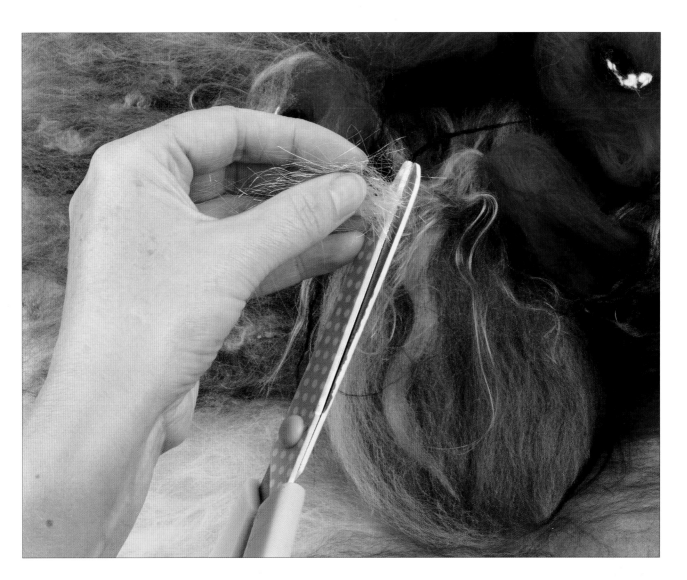

25 Take a small bundle of green Angelina fibres and snip small lengths of them over the green areas of the picture to add some sparkle.

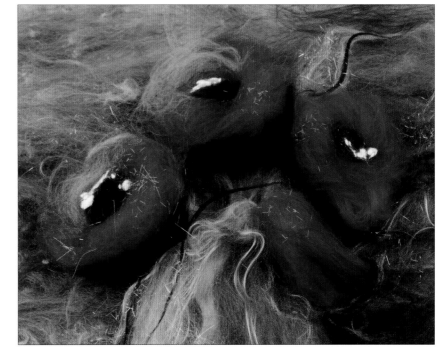

26 Repeat step 25 using red Angelina fibres, sprinkling the snippets over the flowerheads. When you have finished, stand back and assess your picture. Add in more colour and texture if you feel it needs it. You are now ready to felt.

Wet felting

Once your picture is complete you will need to felt it. Felting is the matting together of wool fibres using soap and hot water to form a dense, stable fabric that does not fray. The length of time it will take you to felt will depend on how much pressure you are able to apply. The times given here are a rough guide, but as you practise more and more you will discover for yourself how long you need. The instructions shown here use soap flakes, but guidance is also given if you wish to use olive oil soap, which is commonly available from felt suppliers.

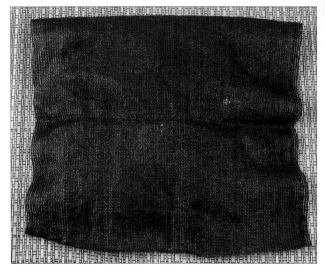

1 Taking care not to disturb the arrangement, lay a piece of netting or plastic mesh over your picture.

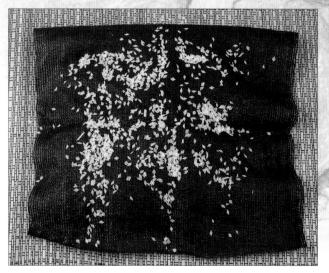

2 Sprinkle on a small amount of soap flakes, if using.

3 Pour some hot water over your picture – use enough to get all the soap flakes wet, but do not completely drench your work. You can always add more water later if you need to. If you are using a bar of olive oil soap rather than flakes, pour on the hot water first, then carefully rub the soap directly onto the plastic mesh to create a lather.

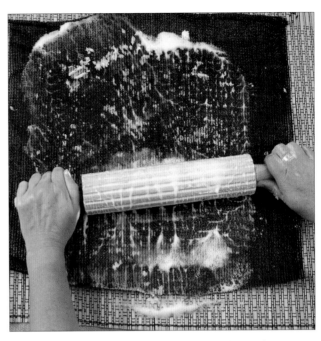

4 Lay one hand flat on the picture to keep the felt in position. With your other hand, rub gently in circular motions all over the picture, lathering up the soap as you go and gradually increasing the pressure. Continue for about ten minutes, until the picture has flattened evenly.

5 Using a ribbed roller, roll all over the picture in different directions, applying as much pressure as possible. Do this for about five to ten minutes. The soap should create a good, thick lather as you work.

6 Using a ridged felting tool and circular motions, continue to apply pressure to the picture. Keep doing this for about five minutes. The change in movement will encourage the fibres to bind strongly together.

7 After you have finished flattening the picture, carefully peel back the netting to reveal the felted picture.

8 Loosely roll up the picture inside the bamboo mat – be careful not to roll it too tightly, or you may cause it to bunch up into ridges.

9 Roll the mat backwards and forwards for two to three minutes – the movement creates friction, which helps to matt the fibres together. It will also squeeze out some of the water and continue to lather up the soap.

10 Carefully unroll the mat, easing the felt off the roll. Turn the picture by 90 degrees, then roll it back inside the mat and repeat step 9. Repeat this process six more times, each time spinning the felt by 90 degrees. The felt is now ready for rinsing.

Tip

If you find applying pressure for long periods of time painful for your wrists and arms, why not transfer the mat to the floor and roll it using your feet?

Rinsing

Rinse the felt, mesh and bamboo mat thoroughly under a cold, running tap to remove all the soap. Squeeze out the excess water from the felt, then transfer it to a bowl of hot water – when you roll the felt for the final time, this will help to strongly bind the fibres together. Again, squeeze the excess water from the felt, then roll it as you did in steps 8–10 using the clean bamboo mat; turn the felt once and re-roll. Allow the felt to dry out thoroughly: hang it on a washing line or on a radiator, or speed up the drying process by ironing it or using a hairdryer.

NEEDLE FELTING

Felting needles are barbed and very sharp – as the needles are pushed through the felt, the barbs catch and entangle the fibres, securing them in place. Use felting needles to hone and refine your felted picture: secure loose fibres and redefine shapes, or add or reposition elements that might have moved during the felting process. To protect your work surface and your felting needles, always work on a piece of dense foam, about 5cm (2in) thick.

Tip

Due to the nature of the felting process, your picture might change slightly and you may want to adapt or add elements – take a step back after felting and reassess it.

I   Use the side of the needle to mould the vase or flowers into shape if they have become wispy or misshapen, then secure the corrected fibres in place – hold the needle vertically and repeatedly stab through the fibres to secure them. Needle felt a thin strand of dark brown merino around the vase's upper left edge.

2   Tease out another thin strand of dark brown merino and needle felt this in place along the line between the yellow and blue background felts.

3   Look for any areas where the felt has shifted slightly – in this case the yellow area to the right of the vase became lower than on the left. Use fine strands of merino to build up or fill in any uneven areas.

4   To create a sense of depth within the picture, add in some dark tones to the left of the vase using very fine pieces of dark brown merino.

5 To make your flowers more vibrant, add some fine wisps of bright pink and scarlet merino to the two left hand flowers, needle felting the fibres into place.

Tip

When applying the different colours, think again about where your imaginary light source is – use the colours to highlight certain areas and bring out the shape of the flowers.

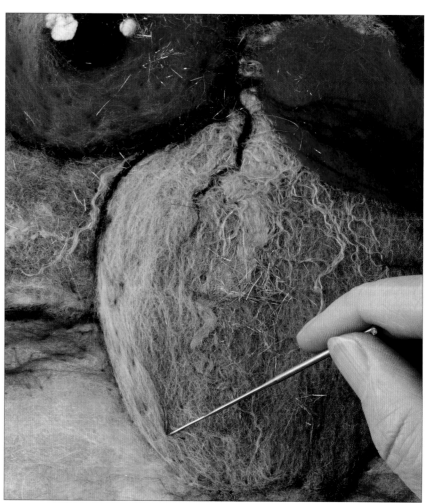

6 To sharpen up the edge, and to inject more colour, needle felt some pale blue merino around the bottom left corner of the vase.

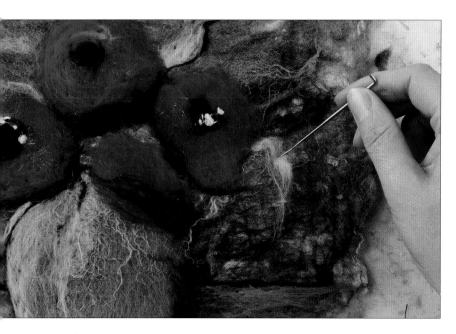

7 If you feel that the balance of your leaves is not quite right, or if they have become too wiggly and wispy, correct them with extra green merino. To the left of the vase, a strand of light green merino has been used to cover a thin-looking leaf; on the vase itself a leaf has been 'filled in' with some new merino, and on the right hand side of the vase an entirely new leaf has been created.

8 As a final touch, needle felt a black oval of merino into the centre of the fourth flower.

Backing

To provide extra support for your stitching and to keep threads and dust from falling into your machine when you come to sew, apply a piece of iron-on interfacing to the back of your picture. Iron the back of your picture first, then lay the interfacing on, adhesive side down. Choose the size of your interfacing depending on how you want your final piece to look: if you plan to trim the edges to neaten the picture, make the interfacing a little bigger all round than your picture; if you plan to leave the outlines uneven and rustic-looking, then make sure that the interfacing is cut smaller all round than your picture. Iron firmly all over using a warm iron.

MACHINE STITCHING

Use machine stitching to add definition and detail to your picture. I use mainly straight stitch, which creates a fine, subtle line ideal for outlining and adding in delicate details. To get the best effects, use free machine embroidery: lower your machine's feed dog and remove the presser foot. This allows you to move the felt around freely under the needle and create flowing, natural lines.

Select your threads based on the effects you want to create – silk threads are shiny and will give a glistening finish whereas cotton threads are matt and more subtle. Generally, I match my top and bobbin threads, but you may want to experiment with using contrasting or complementary bobbin threads, to see what effects you create.

I Set up your machine for free machine embroidery with white thread on the top and in the bobbin. Outline a few of the leaves, defining their sharp tips where the felt may have become wispy. Stitch up and down the leaf veins a few times and sew some thicker areas of stitching around the bases of the leaves.

2 With the white thread still in your machine, outline the flower centres then sew wiggling lines over them, trapping the wool nepps in place as you go. Also sew a few parallel lines of white around the left hand curve of the vase, where you added the extra felt on page 56, to suggest light bouncing off it.

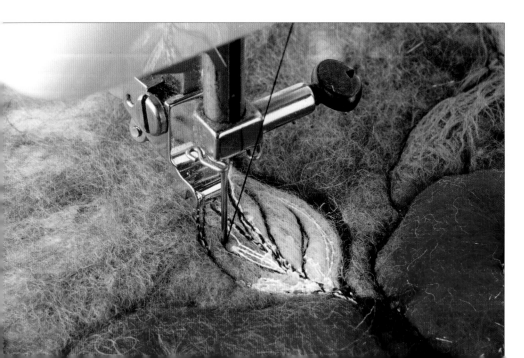

3 Rethread your machine with black top and bobbin thread. Outline all the flowers and any of the leaves that you feel need a bit more definition – here, all except the two leaves on the left were outlined in black. Sew back over some of the leaf veins you created in step 1 and add in a bit more detail if necessary.

4 Sew a few lines around the middle of each flower to suggest the rings of rounded petals. At this point, don't be afraid to keep your stitching fairly simple.

Tip

Remember that your stitching doesn't need to be perfect – uneven, slightly wobbly lines are ideal as they give the work real character.

5 Sew a few wiggling lines over the centre of the flower as you did with white thread in step 2. Create a few short, spiky lines that radiate outwards from the centre.

Tip

You don't need to sew spiky lines right the way round the centre – I find that being selective with the detail you add creates a more interesting effect.

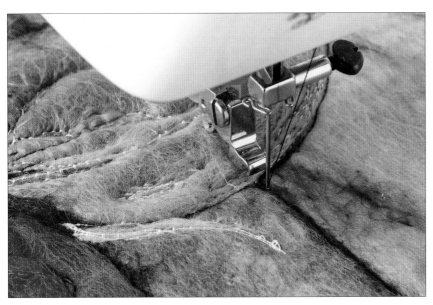

6 Finally, sew around the edge of the vase and along the line between the blue and yellow felts.

Hand stitching

I like to use doubled lengths of embroidery silk when hand sewing – the thick, glossy stitches stand out well against the felt and are great for adding extra splashes of colour to your picture. Unlike machine sewing, these stitches aren't to be used for adding in detail, rather, think of them as dabs of colour that can draw out the highlights within your picture and give it more depth. The stitches I use are simple straight stitches and running stitch. I would advise you to sew a few stitches, then stand back and assess – as with machine sewing, I find that being selective with your stitches creates the most interesting effect.

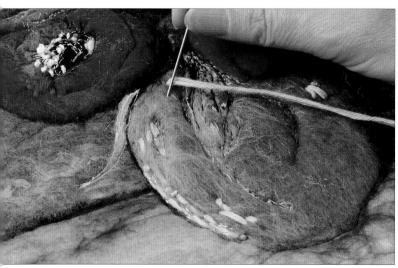

1 Using a doubled length of six-stranded pale blue embroidery thread, sew a mix of long and short straight stitches around the left hand side of the vase. Add in a few extra stitches here and there to add texture, on their own or in groups of two or three.

2 With red thread, sew a mix of long and short stitches on the flowers; radiate them out from the centre, or place them next to the lines of machine stitching. Using white thread, sew small raised dots on the flower centres – work two or three stitches on the same spot.

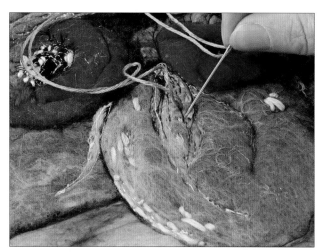

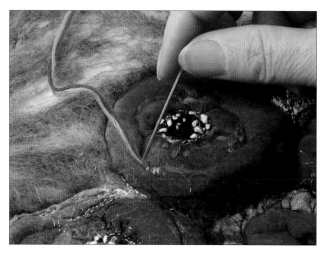

3 Use a green thread to add in some extra detail on the leaves. Sew a few small stitches that follow the direction of the leaves – don't cover the whole surface, just dot the stitches about until you are happy.

4 Using a pink and red blended thread, sew a few last stitches onto the magenta area of the centre top flower – create small raised dots and position them at random to bring out the colour of the felt.

FINISHING

With your picture complete, trim off any excess threads on the front, and secure any loose threads on the back. You can use your finished felting in any number of ways, such as the centrepiece for a special cushion or bag, as the cover for a notebook or simply displayed as a work of art. If you want to, trim the edges carefully using sharp fabric scissors, otherwise leave them looking organic. If you want to display your felting, attach the picture to mounting card using carpet tape under the corners or by stitching through it. It's not advisable to glue the piece, as the glue might seep through and spoil it. Box frames work well, for trimmed or untrimmed pieces, as they won't squash your work.

ESSENTIAL FLOWER FORMS

In this section I will guide you step by step through eight basic flower shapes and show you how to create eight common leaf shapes. I have chosen a mixture of shapes, colours and styles in order to demonstrate the variety of techniques required. Once you have mastered the basic principles for each one you can then transfer them into your still life projects: the methods can easily be adapted to any flowers you choose. I created these flowers on bright, bold backgrounds so that they stand out and I added the Latin names for each of the flowers for reference and to add an extra dimension to them. Generally I stitch words into my feltings in the form of my signature, as well as when working on more architectural pieces – shop signage primarily – which adds another element to the work.

Tulipa, tulip, see pages 76–77.

Bellis perennis, daisy, pages 64–65.

Silybum marianum, thistle, pages 78–81.

Ranunculus, Persian buttercup, pages 74–75.

Lavandula, lavender, pages 72–73.

Papaver somniferum, poppy, pages 70–71.

Viola, pansy, pages 66–69.

Helianthus annuus, sunflower, pages 82–83.

DAISY

 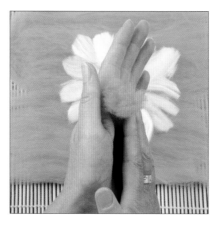 

1 Prepare your backing felt (see page 44). Using white merino and a blend of white and black, cut slightly irregular petal shapes and arrange them as shown above.

2 Roll a chunk of yellow merino between your hands until its cross section becomes a circle.

3 Holding on to the end you want to use, cut a piece about 1cm (½in) thick and place it carefully in the centre of the daisy, so that the cut fibres point upwards.

4 Mlx together a few white and yellow fibres, cut them to form a semi-circle, and lay this on the top half of the daisy centre.

5 Take a small bunch of yellow bamboo fibres in one hand and carefully cut them so that small chunks fall onto the centre of the daisy. Place some white wool nepps on the top right of the centre.

6 Tease out a few wisps of grey merino and carefully place these between some of the petals and on top of others to create the impression of shadow – make sure the darkest areas are towards the centre of the flower. Wet felt following the instructions on pages 52–54.

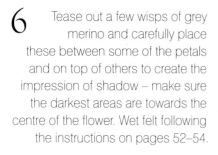 

7   Place your felted fabric onto a thick foam pad. To create a more three-dimensional feel and the illusion of shadow, needle felt a small curve of orange merino around the bottom of the daisy's centre.

8   Tease out thin strands of black merino and use these to outline the centre of the daisy and about half of the petals. Needle felt a few fine strands on top of the orange merino applied in step 7.

9   Prepare for free machine embroidery and use a black thread on the top and in the bobbin. Outline the petals and sew a few short lines up the centre of each. Sew small wiggles of stitching around the bottom of the daisy centre, then finish off with a few in the top right.

10   Rethread your machine with white thread and sew further lines of stitching up the length of the petals, keeping inside the black outlines. Fill in any gaps in the white petal felt with blocks of stitching, and sew a few small white squiggles onto the centre.

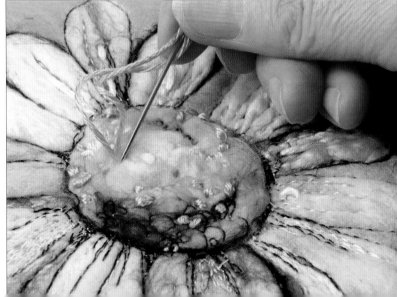

11   Hand sew a few lines of white stitching up the centre of some of the petals, and sew some yellow stitches dotted about all over the centre of the daisy. Depending on how chunky you want them to be, you might want to sew a few stitches on top of each other.

PANSY

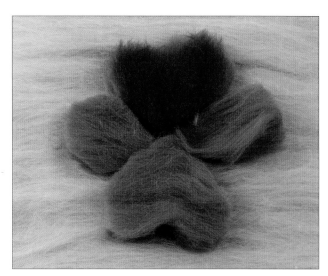

1 Prepare your backing felt. Shape some indigo merino into a 1cm (½in) thick sheet and cut out some petals: cut two oval shapes and two slightly larger heart shapes.

2 Arrange the petals as shown above. Cut a thin layer of deep blue-purple merino to the size of the uppermost petal and place it on top.

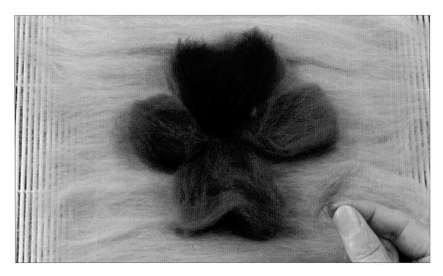

3 Tease out some dark purple merino fibres and use them to create some subtle areas of shading on the three lower petals: place the fibres around the base and up the sides of the petals.

4 Tease out some yellow merino fibres and position them on the upper half of the bottom petal, so that they point down and outwards from the centre of the flower. Mix together some fine strands of lemon yellow and white and position these on the other three petals, radiating out from the centre.

5 Tease out some fine strands of lilac merino and position around the edges of the top three petals. Take three small tufts of black merino and arrange them in the centre of the flower as shown.

6 Cut a small circle of yellow silk and place this in the centre of the flower so that it covers the top of the central black tuft. Add a few white wool nepps above it.

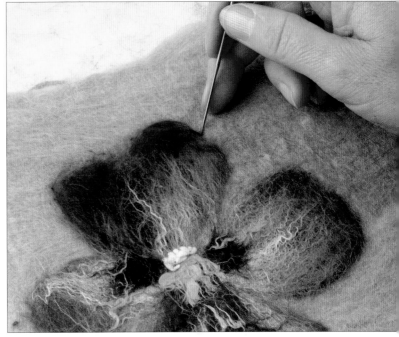

7 Snip some short, thin strands of yellow silk and place these on the bottom three petals so that they radiate out from the centre of the flower. These will give the flower some extra texture. Wet felt following the instructions on pages 52–54.

8 Place the felted fabric onto a thick foam pad. Neaten any edges that have softened or become fuzzy: use the needle to drag the strands into the correct place and then needle felt them into position.

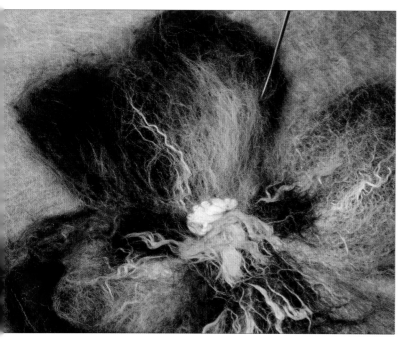

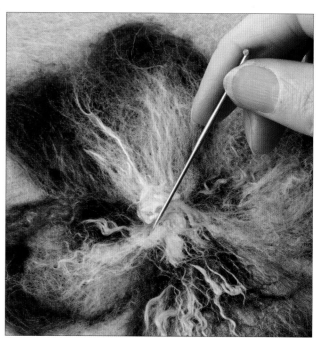

9 If your colours have shifted or faded at all during the felting process, replace them by needle felting extra strands onto the desired areas: here extra yellow merino fibres were added on the right of the top petal.

10 Mix together some yellow and white merino fibres, position them so that they run vertically down the centre of the top petal, and needle felt them on. Add thin strands of white to the centre of the two middle petals.

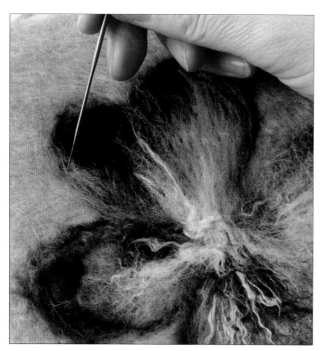

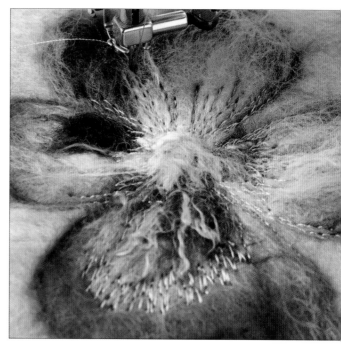

11 Needle felt some strands of lilac around the edges of the top petal to give it more definition.

12 Prepare your machine for free machine embroidery with gold-coloured thread on the top and white in the bobbin. Sew short, straight lines radiating from the centre; on the bottom petal, start the stitching below the area of yellow fibres. Stitch a short way across the two middle petals and sew about half way up the top petal.

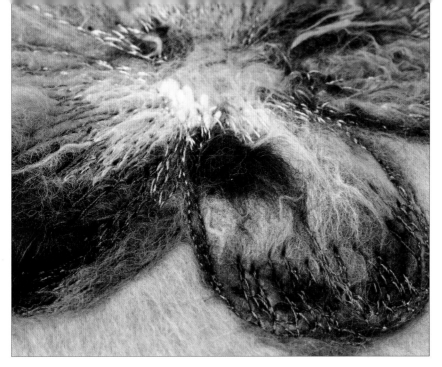

13 Rethread your machine with purple thread and outline each of the petals with a single line of stitches. On the tips of the two middle petals, sew a series of gently curving lines coming in from the edge to about as far as the yellow or white areas. On the top and bottom petals, sew short straight lines that continue to radiate out from the ends of the gold lines created in step 12.

14 Using a white thread, add in some final stitching: sew straight white lines radiating out from the centre across all four petals.

15 Use doubled white embroidery silk to create a few short straight stitches that radiate out from the top of the centre. In the centre itself, create raised white dots by overlaying several stitches on top of each other, then repeat using yellow thread. Finally, on the bottom petal, sew some short, vertical yellow lines on top of the yellow area.

POPPY

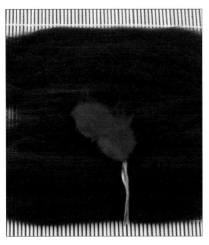

1   Prepare your backing felt. Twist together strands of light and mid-green merino to create the poppy stalk and lay this down. Cut a single petal shape from red merino and position on top of the stalk. Lay a few thin purple fibres on top.

2   Create two more petal shapes from red merino – cut them so that the fibres will lie pointing outwards from the centre of the poppy. Position them on the picture, overlapping the petals slightly.

3   To create some extra texture and colour, add a few strands of pink merino to the right of the top flower, and some red silk strands on the top and bottom petal. Create a ball of black merino and push this into the centre of the flower.

4   Sprinkle some black wool nepps on the centre of the flower and over the base of the top petal. Place a few white wool nepps on as well, keeping them within the centre. Wet felt following the instructions on pages 52–54.

5   Place the felted fabric onto a thick foam pad. Use a felting needle to neaten any edges that have become wispy. For extra colour, add some fine strands of orange to the edges of the top petal.

6 Sometimes the felting process can cause elements such as the wool nepps to come free of your picture. Don't worry if this happens: simply needle felt on some tiny balls of merino to replace them.

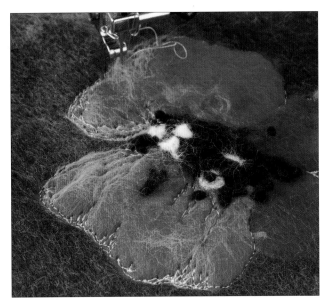

7 Prepare your sewing machine for free machine stitching, with orange thread in the top and white in the bobbin. Sew around the outside of each of the petals and in places sew lines or areas of stitching pointing inwards, to give the impression of a crinkled texture.

8 Rethread your machine with black thread. Sew a wiggling pattern over the poppy centre to secure the wool nepps in place. Outline the stem and each of the petals, creating a few inward-pointing lines and areas of stitching, as in step 7. Create stamens by sewing circle-topped lines protuding up from the centre.

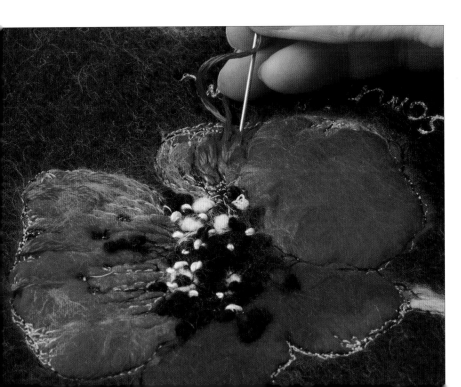

9 Using doubled white embroidery thread, create a scattering of raised dots in the poppy centre by overlaying several stitches on top of each other. With doubled red thread, sew a few straight stitches pointing inwards from the petal edges.

LAVENDER

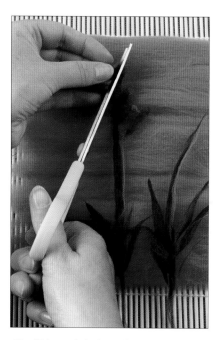

1   Prepare your backing felt. From a variety of different greens, tease out some thin strands – two for the stalks and about twelve for the leaves. Twist the ends of each to a point. Arrange them as shown, adding a thin line of light green merino on the right of the stems.

2   Take a tight bundle of purple merino in your hand and cut small, pointed snippets from it, allowing them to fall over the top of the left hand stem. Repeat the process using a lighter, lilac merino.

3   Twist some tiny green pieces of merino into tight strands and position four of them along the upper part of the second stem.

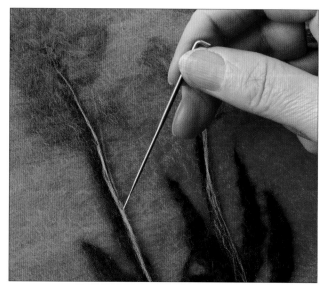

4   Place a thin piece of lilac merino on top of a thin piece of purple merino and roll them together to create a spiral cross section. Cut thin spiral pieces and position them on the second stem. Cut off some extra snippets to fill out the flower shapes. Wet felt following the instructions on pages 52–54.

5   Place the felted fabric onto a thick foam pad. Use a felting needle to neaten any edges that have become wispy. If you feel that your colours aren't quite strong enough, add on some more merino. Here, I added another strand of light green merino to the length of the stems and on the edges of the leaves.

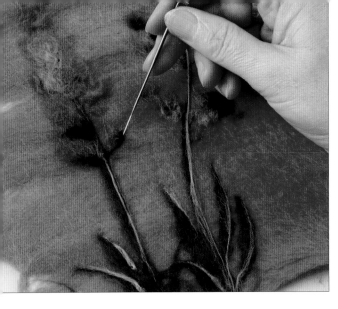

6 To make your flowers look more three-dimensional, and to create some extra definition if your shapes have softened, add in a few small areas of dark purple and black; only use black around the base of the flowers.

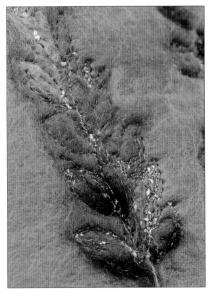

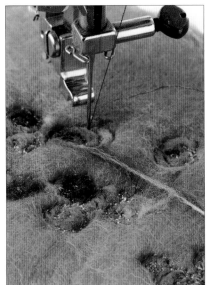

7 Prepare your sewing machine for free machine stitching, with purple thread in the top and white in the bobbin. Sew up the centre of the left flowerhead, branching off on either side to create the flowerbuds.

8 Sew small spirals on top of the flowers on the right hand stem.

9 Rethread your machine with pale green thread and outline the stems and all the leaves – create sharp points at the leaf tips.

10 Using a doubled length of light purple embroidery thread, sew some short, straight stitches up the right hand side of the flowers on the left stem, pointing them outwards at a slight angle. On the right hand stem, using a darker purple thread, create dots on some of the flowers by overlaying several stitches on top of each other.

Persian buttercup

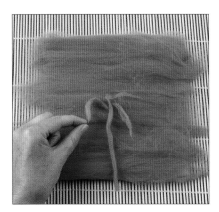

1 Prepare your backing felt. Tease out strands of green merino and create a stem and three leaves.

2 Pull together some white and lemon yellow merino so that the fibres all sit in the same direction.

3 Roll the blended fibres loosely around your finger.

4 Remove the fibres from your finger, being careful to keep the spiral intact as you do so. Tease out a second piece of white and yellow merino and wrap this around the rolled piece to continue the spiral; manipulate it so that it forms a neat, rose-like shape.

5 Place the flowerhead on top of the stem, angling it slightly so that the centre of the spiral is facing upwards but is still visible from the front.

6 Tease out some thin yellow silk fibres and position them around the flower so that they follow the shape of the spiral and highlight its shape. Also lay some darker yellow and brown merino fibres around the bottom edge of the flower.

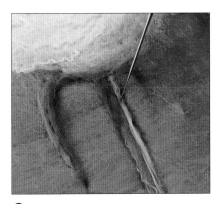

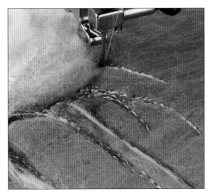

7 As in step 6, add some thin white silk strands following the spiral of the petals. Tease out thin strands of dark green merino and place under the petals and down the stem. Add a ball of dark brown merino in the centre. Wet felt following the instructions on pages 52–54.

8 Place the felted fabric onto a thick foam pad. Use the felting needle to neaten up any edges that have become wispy. If your colours have faded at all, add some new merino on top: here, I added light green strands to the stem and leaves.

9 Prepare your sewing machine for free machine embroidery, with green thread in the top and white in the bobbin. Outline the stem and leaves and fill in any areas of green that may look a little bit gappy.

10 Using a yellow top thread, outline the flower and then sew in the details of the petals: these flowers have a very intricate, tightly packed petal structure, so reflect this by sewing close, wiggly lines of stitching that spiral outwards from the centre.

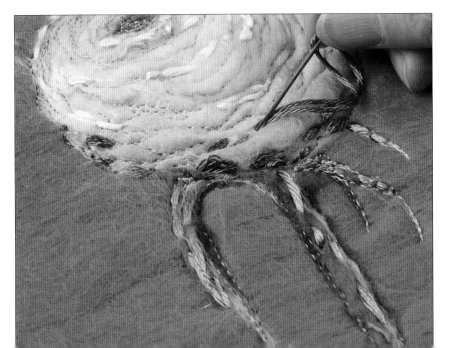

11 Add in a few long and short straight stitches of doubled green embroidery silk up the stem and along the leaves. Use white and brown threads on the flowerhead: use brown around the bottom and white closer to the top – roughly follow the lines of machine stitching.

TULIP

1 Prepare your backing felt. Take a strand of light green merino and a strand of mid-green merino and twist them together to make a stem.

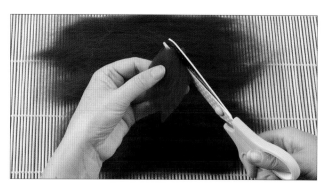

2 Tease out a piece of red-purple merino to an even thickness and cut out a pointed petal shape.

3 Lay down the stem in position. Cut three further petals, each from a different pink merino – make two of these the same size as the first and make one slightly smaller, as this will half-cover one of the full-size petals. Twist the tops of each to get a sharp, tulip-like shape.

4 Layer the petals as shown on top of the stem, with the lightest at the back, half-covered with the smallest petal shape, and the darkest at the front.

5 Add on silk highlights for extra texture: place pink strands on the petals and a green strand on the stem. Also add some wisps of bright pink merino to the darkest petal. Wet felt following the instructions on pages 52–54.

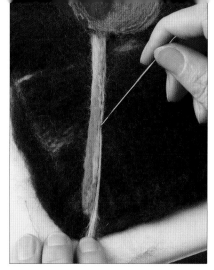
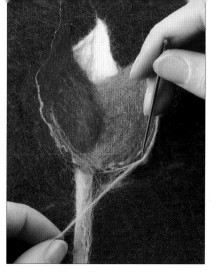
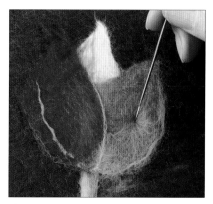

6 Place the felted fabric onto a thick foam pad. Use the felting needle to neaten any wispy edges. To give some extra definition, needle felt a thin line of white merino down the right hand side of the stem.

7 Apply another thin strand of white merino around the right hand side of the flower and up between the front two petals.

8 To create more depth of tone, tease out a few fine wisps of lilac merino and needle felt these on to the lower portion of the right hand petal.

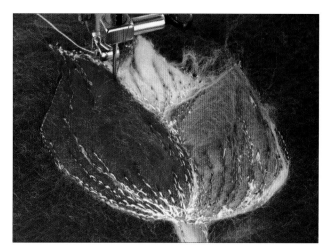

9 Prepare your sewing machine for free machine embroidery, with white thread in the top and in the bobbin. Outline the stem and all the petals then add in some detail: sew short, curving lines up the centre of each petal, following the shape of the flower.

10 Rethread your machine with pink thread and re-outline the petals. Create more curving lines up the centre of the petals and 'sketch' in areas at the tips.

11 Use doubled white embroidery silk to sew a few curved lines of stitching on the pale and mid-pink petals. Using a dark purple embroidery silk, dot some stitches about on the darkest two petals, to complement your machine stitches.

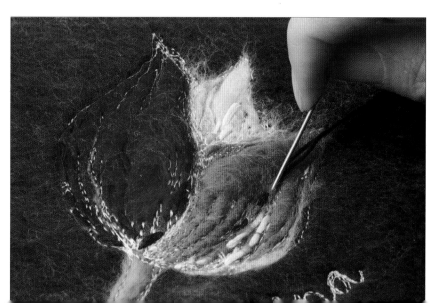

THISTLE

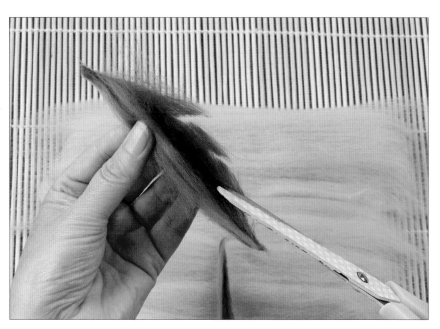

I   Prepare your backing felt. To make a stem, twist together thin strands of light and dark green merino and position on the background felt.

2   Mix together some more light and dark green merino, manipulate it to an even thickness and cut out a pointed leaf shape. Twist the ends to encourage them to form sharp points. Using a pair of scissors, cut small, angled notches down both sides of the leaf.

3   Position the leaf on the backing felt. Carefully twist all the notches to form neat points. Curve the top of the leaf upwards.

4   Cut a rounded chunk of green merino to form the base of the flowerhead. Position this on the top of the stem.

5 Cut a chunk of lilac merino. Holding the piece firmly at one end, splay out the fibres on the top and twist them into points to create the look of a spiky thistle.

6 Position the purple flower; tuck the bottom of the purple under the green base, evenly spreading out the purple spikes against the background.

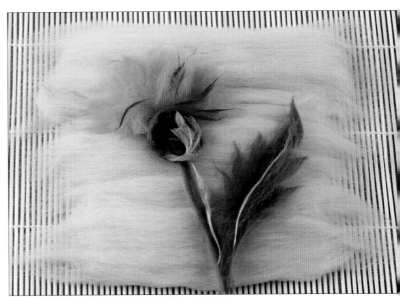

7 Using thin strands of green silk, add highlights to the base of the flowerhead, the stem and the leaf. Try to think about the way the light could be hitting the flower, and position the silk accordingly.

8 Create a few very thin twists of dark purple silk and arrange these on the purple flower. Wet felt following the instructions on pages 52–54.

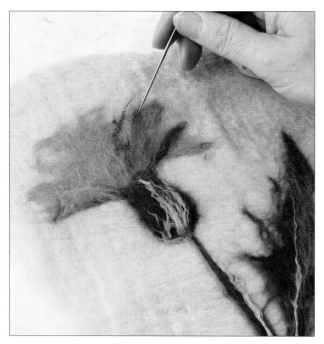

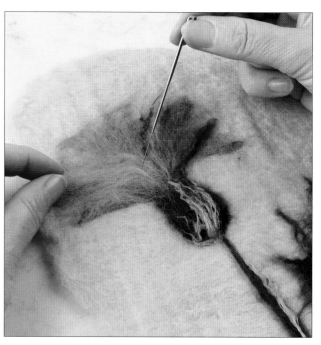

9 Place the felted fabric onto a thick foam pad. Use the felting needle to neaten any areas that have become very wispy. To bring the flower to life, needle felt some thin wisps of pink merino onto the right hand side, following the direction of the spikes.

IO Also add on some wisps of pale blue merino, this time to the left hand side of the flower, again following the direction of the spikes. Finally, add a thin strand of white around the bottom and right hand side of the green base of the flower.

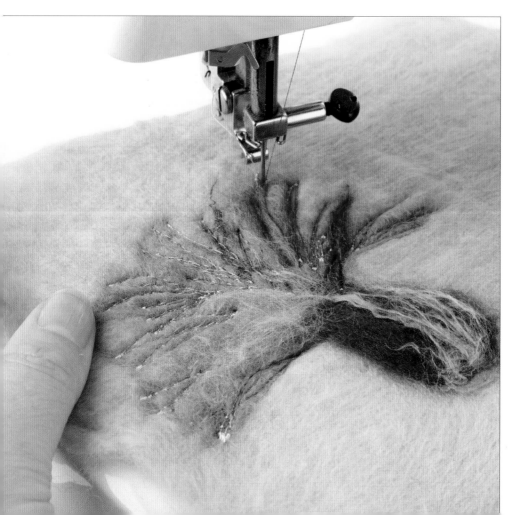

II Prepare your machine for free machine embroidery with pink top and bobbin thread. Starting at the bottom of the flower, sew up to the ends of the spikes, creating slightly curving lines. When you get to the top, leave the needle in the fabric and spin it 180 degrees so that you can sew straight back down the same line to the base, creating a sharp, clean point at the tip. Repeat this all over the flower.

12 Rethread your machine with pale green thread. Outline the stem and leaf and then add in all the leaf veins. Start at the bottom of the leaf and sew upwards, branching out from the centre as you go to create the veins. Finally, sew the base of the flowerbud by outlining it and then sewing lines of zizag stitches across its width to create a diamond-like pattern.

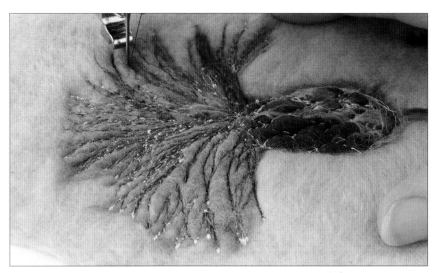

13 Rethread your machine with purple thread and sew in a similar way to step 11: sew sharp, curved lines that radiate out from the base of the flower, but this time, don't be afraid to stop half way before turning back or add in some sharp zigzags of stitching at the tips of the spikes – depending on what you feel your picture needs.

14 Finally, using doubled lengths of pink, purple and lilac embroidery silks, sew lines of running stitch that follow the lines of machine stitching.

SUNFLOWER

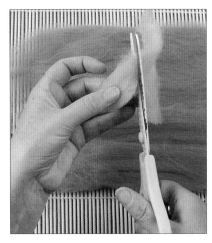

1 Prepare your backing felt. From a variety of yellow and yellow-orange mixed merinos, cut out a number of petal shapes. In this example, fifteen were used.

2 Twist the end of each petal to create a sharp point, then arrange the petals in a double-layered ring, as shown.

3 For some additional colour and texture, place some strands of yellow silk on top of the upper petals.

4 Twist together a chunk of some orange and brown merino fibres, then snip small pieces of this into the centre of the sunflower. Try to get a good mix of colours as you cut.

5 Scatter a few black and white wool nepps onto the sunflower's centre – scatter the black pieces all over but keep the white towards the centre. Wet felt following the instructions on pages 52–54.

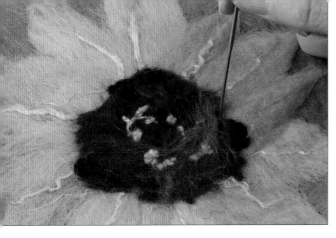

6 Place the felted fabric onto a thick foam pad. To make the sunflower centre look rounded, needle felt a few extra wisps of orange merino around the bottom edge.

7 Use the felting needle to neaten any edges that have become very wispy – you want the petals to retain their sharply pointed tips. Using thin strands of dark brown merino, outline a few of the petals to give some extra definition and a sense of shadow and depth.

8 Prepare your machine for free machine embroidery, with black top and bobbin thread. Outline each of the petals and sew a line or lines up the centre of each to about the half or three-quarter point. Sew over the centre of the flower in a random, wiggling pattern.

9 Rethread your machine with orange thread. As you did in step 8, sew a short way up the centre of a few of the petals, then sew a wiggling pattern over the lower part of the sunflower centre.

10 Using doubled lengths of white and then brown embroidery thread, create raised dots all over the centre of the sunflower by sewing a couple of stitches on top of each other to form each dot.

Basic leaf shapes

As with flowers, leaves come in a wonderful array of shapes, colours and sizes, and making them as detailed and life-like as possible can really enrich your work. Practise using the different techniques shown here – you can then adapt them to make any leaf shape you need.

Mix together light and dark green merino fibres by hand. From this blended merino, cut five pointed leaf shapes and create a stem and branches. After felting, needle felt some darker central veins up the middle of each leaf. Using a pale green thread, machine sew the outlines of the leaves and the stems and add in the leaf veins.

Use carded dark and light green merino to create a stem and long, pointy-ended leaf. After felting, needle felt a thin white strand up the centre of the leaf, then machine sew the outline and leaf veins using pale green thread.

To create the rich tones of this leaf, layer up lots of different green merino fibres and apply some thin silk strands for the leaf veins. After felting, use your machine stitching to bring the leaf to life, adding in elaborate vein patterns and edging.

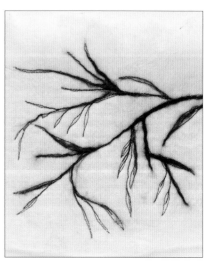

Create the main stems by felting thin strands of dark green merino onto your background in a jagged, branch-like arrangement. Once felted, outline all the stems and add in extra leaves and stems with fine lines of dark stitching.

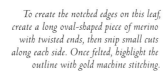

Start by teasing out a thin strand of green merino for the stem. To create the leaves, cut thin widths of green merino and position them leading off the stem with the cut fibres pointing upwards. Once felted, the leaf edges will be very soft, irregular shapes — when you machine sew, trace this zigzag with your stitching to create a wiggly, notched effect.

Cut these heart-shaped leaves from green merino, and once felted, needle felt thin strands of contrasting colours around the edge and down the centre of each. Machine sew the decorative leaf veins using light green thread.

For simpler branch shapes, felt a few strands of dark green merino onto your background, then add in all the detail when you machine sew: create short, spindly branches that emerge from the sides and ends of the stems or, on thicker stems, sew tiny, thorn-like spikes.

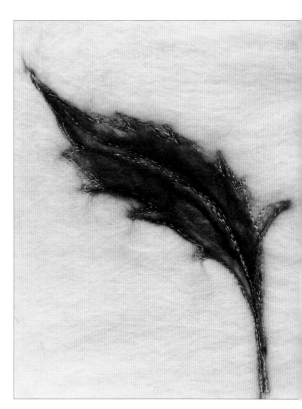

To create the notched edges on this leaf, create a long oval-shaped piece of merino with twisted ends, then snip small cuts along each side. Once felted, highlight the outline with gold machine stitching.

FLOWER STUDY

If you are interested in creating large, detailed flower portraits, a good way to practise is to create flower studies worked directly onto a plain background – early Victorian flower studies offer inspiration for this type of work. Not only are these studies striking and beautiful in their own right, but the emphasis is on the form, structure and detail of the flower – allowing you to focus on the finer detail of the flower without having to consider other elements of the composition. Follow the example given here, or substitute it with your own favourite flowers: use the essential flower form guides on pages 62–85 for inspiration.

Layering the fibres and composing the picture

1 Work out what your colour and fibre palette will be: here, the background is white merino and the flowers are created from blue, green, purple, pink and grey merinos, with some additional green silk fibres.

2 Prepare a piece of white background felt following the instructions on page 44. Take some uncarded dark green merino and create thin strands by pulling the merino apart along its length, as shown.

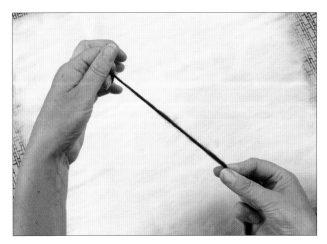

3 Twist each strand of merino between your fingers to bind the fibres together and create neat ends.

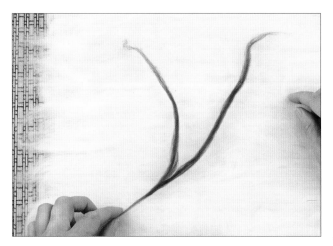

4 Lay down two strands of green merino to form the stems of the plant. Twist the two ends together.

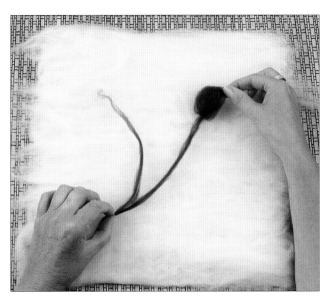

5 Create an oval-shaped ball of green merino, ensuring that the ends are neatly tucked away. Position the ball so that it slightly overlaps the top of the right hand stem.

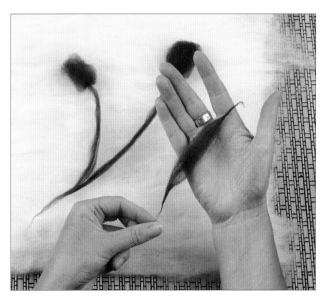

6 Create a second ball and place this on top of the left hand stem. Cut a thick strand of green merino and twist both ends so that it forms a neat leaf shape.

Using different greens and greys, create about seven more leaves of varying sizes and position these along the two stems. Try to space them evenly, with the largest at the bottom and the smallest at the top. Twist them as you lay them down, and curve some of the ends up or down for a natural look.

Create some thin strands of light green merino and lay them along the right hand side of the stems to give the impression of light hitting the plant.

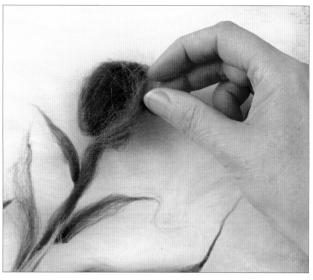

9   Tease out a few strands of light green merino and place them on the right hand side of each of the green balls. Apply the fibres as though you were painting with watercolours, building up thin layers of colour.

10   To complete the green elements, add thin strands of light green silk to the stems and the tops of the leaves. Also add strands of dark green or grey to the undersides of some of the leaves. Remember to consider your imagined light source while doing so.

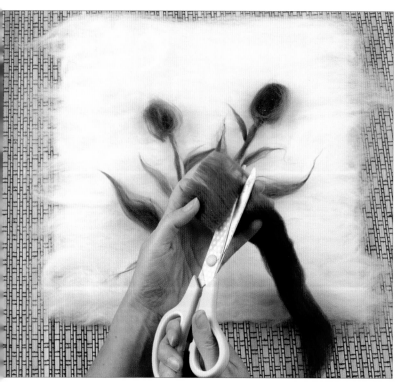

12   Holding one end of the piece securely, twist sections of the loose fibres into points.

11   Cut horizontally across a strip of purple merino.

13 Place the flower at the top of the right stem, tucking the end under the green ball. Add a small thin strand of green silk on the right of the ball. To create the second flower, mix some light and dark purple merino fibres and create the flower following steps 11 and 12.

14 Position the second flower on the picture. Make sure that you are happy with the arrangement of the spikes on both flowers. Pull a few of the spikes forwards slightly so that they lie on top of the green ball.

15 From both light and dark purple fibres, create a few small, tight twists of merino.

16 Position the short coloured twists on the right hand flower, tucking them in amongst the existing fibres; place the dark ones to the right and the light ones to the left. Wet felt following the instructions on pages 52–54.

Needle felting

17 Place the felted fabric onto a thick foam pad. If some of the fibres have shifted about slightly during the felting process, it may be possible to lift them off and reposition them with the needle. Redefine any edges that have become wispy or very uneven.

18 Some fibres, especially those such as silks, which tend to sit on the surface of the felt, can pucker and become wiggly during the felting process. If you want to, pull these straight and needle felt in place.

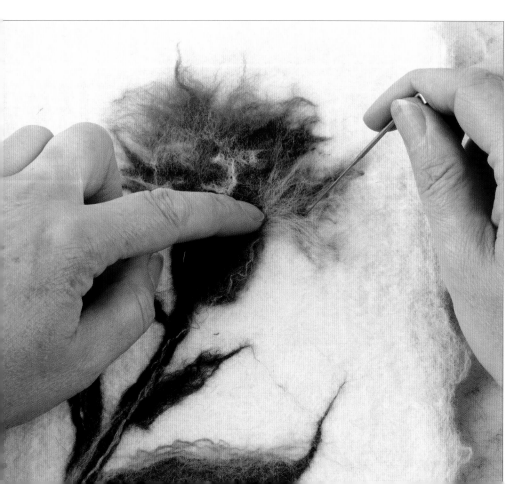

19 To brighten your flowers, tease out some fine blue merino fibres and needle felt them onto the right hand flower, following the direction of the spikes.

Machine stitching

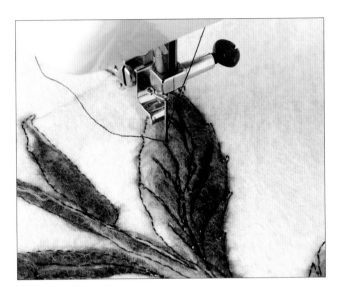

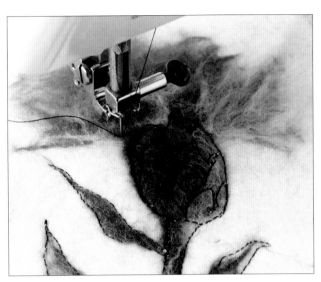

20 Prepare your machine for free machine embroidery, with black top and bobbin thread. Outline the stems and all the leaves; on a few of the larger leaves, create a slightly jagged, notched outline. Draw in the leaf veins on a few of the larger leaves.

21 Sew the base of the flowerhead by outlining the shape then sewing horizontal lines of zigzag stitches across it to create a diamond-like pattern.

22 Your stitching on the flowers should follow the direction of the spikes: for the flower on the right, draw in spikes that radiate up from the base of the flower. For the flower on the left, allow some of the spikes to fall forwards; create spikes going both up and down.

23 Rethread your machine with pink thread. Sew a small area of pink spikes on each flowerhead.

Hand stitching

24 Using doubled lengths of pale green and blended green embroidery silks, sew lines of running stitch up the stems and part way up the centre of the largest leaves. Dot a few small stitches about on the base of the flowerheads: scatter the stitches about at random – they do not all need to point in the same direction.

25 To finish off the flowers, sew in some lines of running stitch, following your machine-sewn spikes. Use dark purple, lilac and pink threads to add a burst of colour.

FLOWERS IN STILL LIFE

In my experience, the best results come from real-life setups. When you have a vase of flowers in front of you it's possible to study them from all angles, pick them up, closely examine details such as the directions of the veins, the variation in colours within each petal, and the inner detail. Give thought to colour combinations, patterns and shapes when choosing your background: lace, saris, checks and tartans make for interesting additions, as does the choice of your vase or vessel. Think outside the box; try using differently shaped and patterned vases, bottles, jugs, and even teapots to hold the flowers in. The more interesting the composition at this stage the more interesting the end result is likely to be. Be courageous. Include items that you find meaningful, inspiring and exciting. There is so much joy to be had from taking an object you love and using it to create something new and exciting. When your still life set up is aesthetically pleasing to your eye, you are ready to start. You should find that this initial care and preparation will make the actual painting process happier and more straightforward.

....
Lilacs with Pear
37 x 37cm (14¹/₂ x 14¹/₂in)
Try combining unusual objects when setting up still life compositions. The randomness can make for a more interesting, sometimes quirky end result.

Tangerine Blue

36 x 36cm (14¼ x 14¼in)

I love putting complementary shades of blue and orange together — the vibrant tangerines look really striking against the blues used for the background and flowers. I kept the background fairly plain here as I wanted the white tin jug to stand out, and thin webs of merino were added at the end to create more shadow.

Periwinkle Blues

40 x 32cm (16 x 12½in)

*I approached this piece in a fairly abstract manner,
concentrating more on the placement of colour than the
definite shapes of the flowers. I like the freeness of this piece.*

White Cat and Lilacs

40 x 40cm (16 x 16in)

*Against a dark background I have added my white cat.
I wanted to keep the cat simple and without too many
features so that the main focus was the flowers. I am
happy with how the two elements work together here.*

The Spotty Tablecloth

30 x 27cm (12 x 11in)

This piece demonstrates that even with relatively little embellishment you can still achieve an interesting and attractive felting. I chose to add just small amounts of stitching to some of the flowers at the front — which draws the eye — leaving the ones behind relatively untouched.

Reds on Black

35 x 24cm (14 x 9½in)

Using vibrant silks and Angelina fibres on a dark background colour allows the delicate shapes and patterns of the flowers to stand out well, making them the focus of the piece.

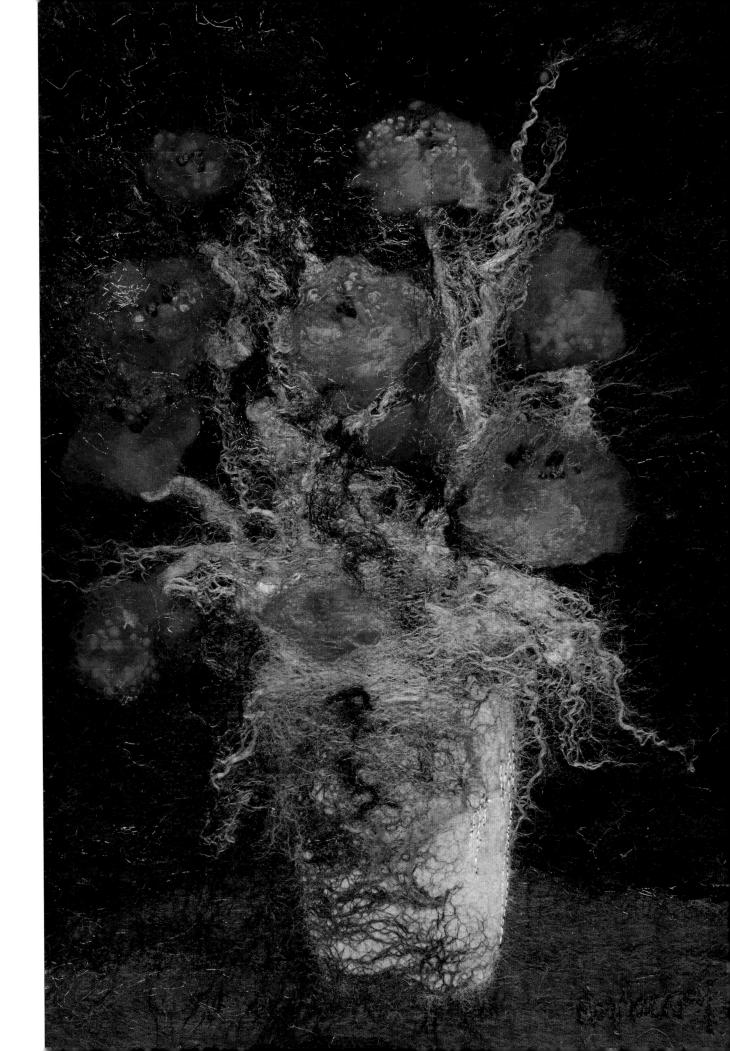

The Blue Jug

30 x 26cm (12 x 10¼in)

*Working directly onto a solid background colour allows
the eye to focus better on the detail of the flowers. Often
the simpler the piece, the most striking it is.*

Roses, Violets and Lilacs

35 x 25cm (14 x 10in)

*Using a dark background and simple vase shape helps
to emphasise the vibrancy and textures of the flowers,
leaves and stems.*

Still life project

In this project I have chosen items that have relatively simple shapes – all can be moulded in your hands or cut out with scissors. I find that it is best to concentrate on capturing basic outlines first, as you can later add more detail in the stitching; it will be during this process of embellishment that you can refine the detail and take the work to another level. To make the piece more personal, why not substitute other flowers for the tulips, or swap in other simple shapes in place of the bowl of cherries?

Layering the fibres and composing the picture

I Select your colour and fibre palette: here, the top half of the background is carded blue and green; the lower half is blue with a grey overlay. The rest of the picture uses a rainbow of merino, from red cherries and a blue vase to pink and yellow tulips. Blue silk noil, white wool nepps and Angelina fibres have also been used to add extra interest.

2 Prepare your backing felt. Cover the top half with tufts of blue-green carded merino. Cover the rest of the white with long horizontal strands of uncarded blue. The difference in the two textures creates a contrasting effect when felted.

3 To give the picture some depth, tease out some fine pieces of dark grey merino and lay them on the top half of the blue merino – don't cover the blue completely; keep the grey thin enough that the blue shows through in places.

4 Create about five leaves and six stems by twisting a blend of light and mid-green fibres into strands; make the leaves fatter than the stems and twist the ends to create neat points. For variety, create some leaves from a mix of greens.

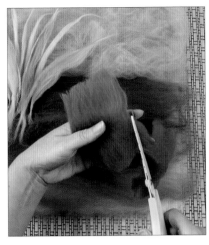

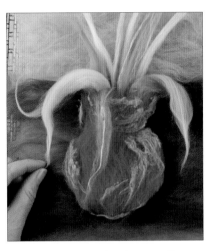

5 Spread out some bright blue merino to an even thickness and cut a rounded vase shape from it. Position it on top of your stems.

6 To make the vase look three-dimensional, use some strands of paler blue silk noil to create highlights: place these on the sides of the vase and around the rim.

7 With the vase in place, pull a few of the leaves down to make them look as though they are bending over the rim of the vase.

8 Card together some strands of white and pink merino and cut out a tulip-shaped flower.

9 Cut two more tulips from the blend of white and pink fibres, and position them on top of three stems.

10 Card together some yellow and white fibres and from this create two more flower shapes. Position them on the picture as shown, with one hanging forward.

11 To give the vase a dotty pattern, place wool nepps all over it, keeping them evenly spaced.

12 To create shade in amongst the leaves, add in some thin strands of dark green merino.

13 Spread out an even piece of blue merino, the same colour as you used for the vase, and cut out a bowl shape. Position this next to the vase.

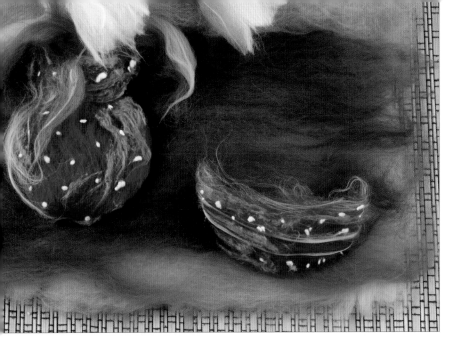

14 Run some very fine strands of light blue silk around the rim of the bowl and then around its centre to create two thin stripes. Also add a line of blue silk down the left hand edge of the vase. Add a few strands of blue silk noil to the left hand side of the bowl, then dot the whole surface with white wool nepps.

15 Card together some red and maroon merino. Tease this out flat and from it cut seven small circles for the cherries. Arrange six in the bowl and stand one next to the vase. Add another strand of pale blue silk to the rim of the bowl, and place a thin strand of green silk behind the single cherry.

16 To create more dramatic tones within the picture, add some strands of hot pink merino to the edges of the pink tulips and some bright yellow strands to the yellow tulips. Also add thin wisps of pink merino to the cherries. Position the merino on one side of each cherry, where it will catch the light.

17 To complete the merino elements of the picture, apply subtle dark and light tones around the shapes: use fine wisps of grey under the bowl; fine white fibres under the bowl, to the left of the vase and up the left hand edge to the top; and dark green on the horizon and around the flowers.

18 Hold a small bunch of red Angelina fibres in one hand and carefully cut small snippets over all the cherries. Repeat the process, snipping blue Angelina fibres over the left hand edges of the vase and bowl, and green Angelina fibres over the background. Wet felt following the instructions on pages 52–54.

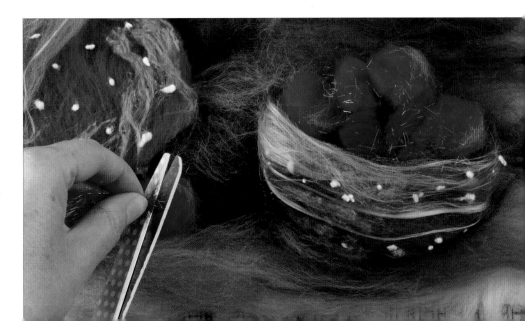

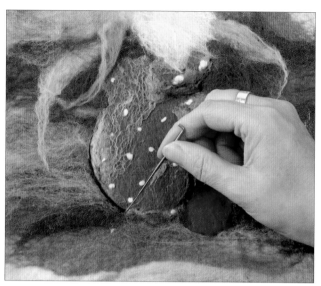

19 Use the felting needle to neaten up any wispy edges and to reposition any elements that have moved. Tease out a few strands of purple merino and wrap these around the sides of some of the cherries to give them a shadow. Needle felt this purple in place.

20 To make the vase stand out from the background, needle felt thin lines of dark blue merino down each side and around the bottom curve. To accentuate the shape, apply a few curved horizontal strands around the indentation on the top right.

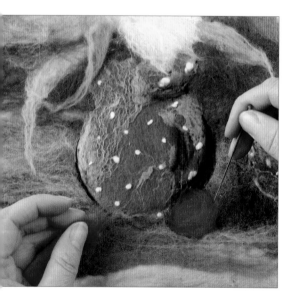

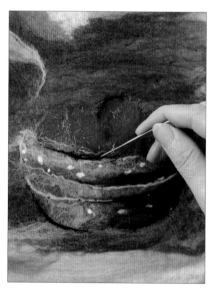

21 Needle felt a few gently curved vertical lines of dark blue on the right hand side of the vase. Add thin wisps of hot pink merino onto the right hand edges of some of the cherries.

22 Needle felt a fine layer of dark blue merino onto the right hand side of the bowl and blend the colour across to about the half way point. Twist some thin strands of black merino, and needle felt these around the rim and around the bottom left hand edge.

23 Using some fine wisps of black or dark grey merino, add some shading around the lower left side of the bowl, to give the impression of a shadow.

24 Apply a thin black line of merino to the underside of any leaves that need definition; add dark green lines on the stems.

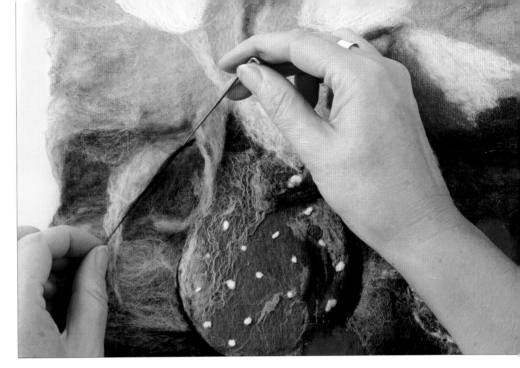

25 Tease out a few strands of hot pink, and needle felt thin stripes on to the pink flowers: use the strands to highlight the gaps between petals and to create striped markings on the outside of the petals.

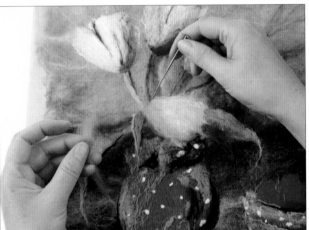

26 Add some subtle shading to the yellow tulips by needle felting some thin strands of orange merino around their bases and along one or both of their edges.

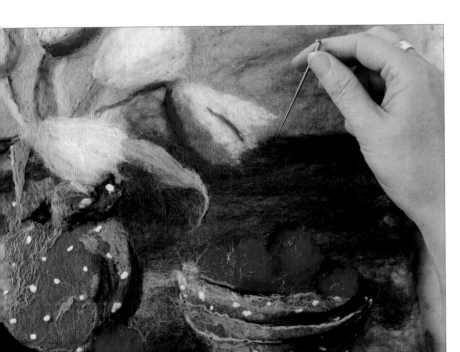

27 Take a look at your horizon line and if it has become uneven or wonky, correct it using dark green merino fibres.

Machine stitching

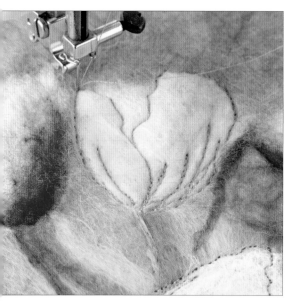 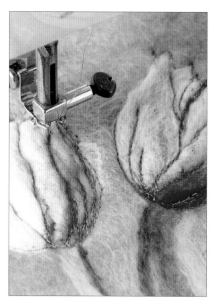 

28 Prepare your machine for free machine stitching with orange top and bobbin thread. Outline the yellow tulips first, dividing the petals with delicate, slightly wiggling lines and drawing short curving lines up from the base.

29 Rethread your machine with dark pink thread and draw in the pink tulips: outline all the flowers and sew in delicate, wiggling dividing lines between the petals before sewing short curving lines up the petals from the base.

30 With the pink still in your machine, outline all the cherries, creating a sketchy effect around their right hand edges to make them look shiny.

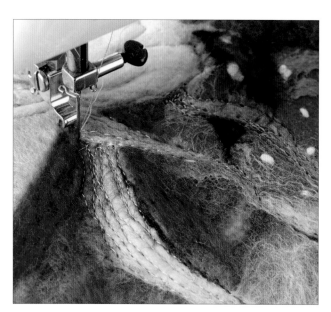 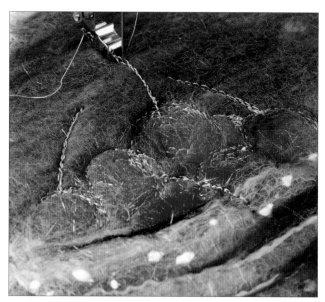

31 Rethread your machine with green thread. Outline all the stems and leaves, sewing parallel lines of green along the length of each leaf and up each stem.

32 Sew short, curved lines to create the stems of the cherries. Sew over the lines a few times so that they are clearly visible.

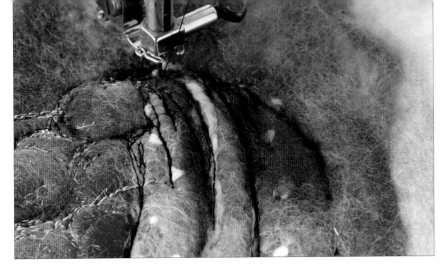

33 Rethread your machine with black thread and sew sketchy lines inwards from the right hand side, following the lines of the rim and the stripes. Outline the bowl and then outline all the cherries within it.

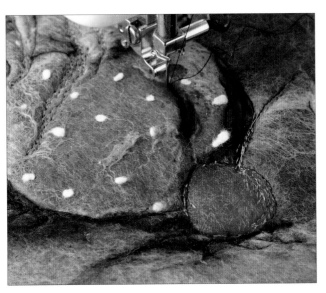

34 With the black thread still in your machine, outline the freestanding cherry and its stalk, then sew over the vertical merino lines you added in step 21.

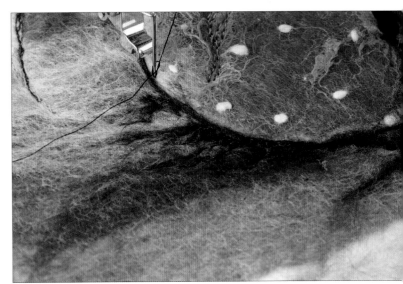

35 Outline the vase, then sew short, sketchy lines outwards into the shadow on the left hand side.

36 Sew sketchy lines into the indentation on the top right of the vase. Add in a few extra lines along the length of the overhanging leaves and up any stems you want to give extra definition to.

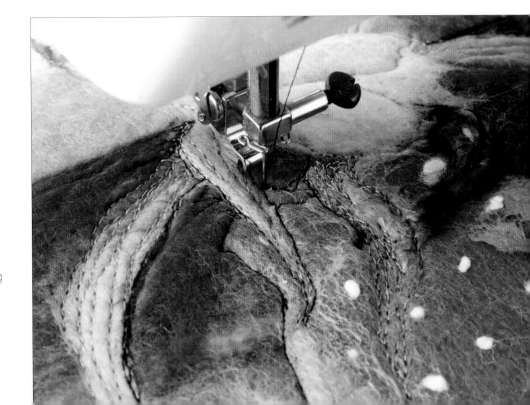

Hand stitching

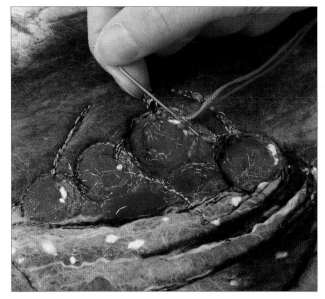

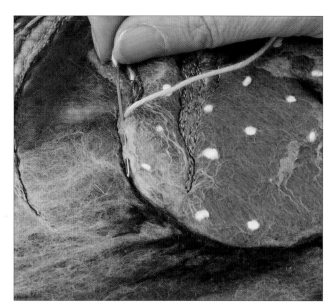

37 Using a doubled length of pink–red blend embroidery silk, sew curved lines of small stitches around the right hand side of the upper cherries and the freestanding cherry. Sew a few white stitches amongst the pink to make the cherries look really glossy.

38 Using a doubled length of light blue thread, sew a few long running stitches down the left hand side of the vase and around the rim.

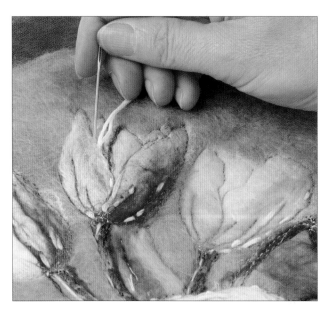

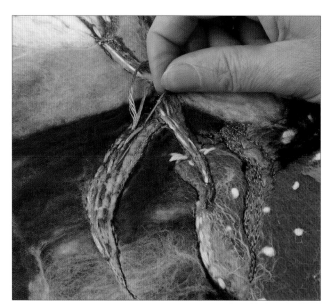

39 Using doubled lengths of light pink thread for the pink tulips and light yellow thread for the yellow tulips, sew broken lines of long and short straight stitches up the lengths of some of the petals.

40 Using a variety of different green threads, sew lines of stitches along some of the leaves and cherry stalks and up the stems.

Finishing

Finish your picture using the guidance on page 61.

FLOWERS IN THE LANDSCAPE

Landscapes are my favourite subject matter. The land around us has a natural energy that is a wonderful challenge to capture, be it dark stormy skies or bright summer meadows. I am lucky to live in a very beautiful part of the world where I find inspiration all around me – I am never without a camera or sketchbook and am constantly documenting scenes I like, whether for the colour combinations or simply for the composition. Often I will marry the two, as there is no benefit to rigidly sticking to one photograph or sketch if you prefer aspects of another. In the examples shown here I have taken structural elements from one source and then either added the flowers from another or simply created them from my imagination. These images are my dream landscapes, where an abundance of brightly coloured flowers grow all around: by using your imagination you can create these magnificently coloured secret gardens and rainbow meadows without limitations. Varying the textures and weights of fibres will give interesting and three-dimensional qualities to your work, and I find that experimenting with different types of traditional and invented embroidery stitches can be particularly satisfying in areas that are dense with flowers.

At Lavender Bothy

15 x 15cm (6 x 6in)

This was a little study, as you can tell by the size of the stitches. Quick small studies are a great means of familiarising yourself with your medium and testing out colour combinations.

Washing Day at Glengaber, Traquair

70 x 70cm (27¼ x 27¼in)

*This large piece was a joy to create. I worked from a photograph,
following the composition and placement of the building, washing
line and trees, but then created the foreground from my imagination.
Adding flower forms and colour was a pleasure and great fun!*

Blue Thatches at Barley Meadow

40 x 40cm (16 x 16in)

*Keeping a large portion of this piece simple, with relatively flat
colours and shapes, allows the flowers in the foreground to be the
main focus. The eye is drawn to the finer detail and colours of the
flowers, accentuated by the plain yellow of the field behind.*

The Holy Isle from Lamlash, The Isle of Arran

60 x 60cm (23 ½ x 23 ½in)

I liked the way the bold shape of the island contrasted with the calm of the surrounding sea, and also how the mix of wild flowers appears to frame the entire view. I wanted to create a painting that included all these aspects rather than simply a sea scene — I feel that the flowers help to ground the piece.

The Secret Garden

48 x 56cm (19¼ x 22in)

This piece is a gallery favourite. By combining darks and lights the piece has taken on a slightly eerie yet uplifting feel. I worked from a photograph but in a very free manner, using it only occasionally as a reference.

LANDSCAPE PROJECT

In this project I have chosen a fairly basic Tuscan composition – this is a good first landscape to try as it is beautiful and inviting but also simple to create. The cypress trees are made by twisting fibres to create slender, organic shapes, while the sunflowers are formed from small snippets and large chunks of merino, embellished with stitching to create a suggestion of their shape and detail. Experiment with a different colour palette or flower type if you want to adapt the scene to your own tastes.

Layering the fibres and composing the picture

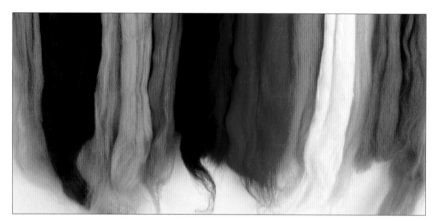

I Select your colour and fibre palette: I used carded white and blue for the sky; a range of greens for the field and the trees; red, white and orange for the buildings; and yellow, orange and brown merino to create the sunflowers. To bring the picture to life I also added green and white silk fibres, green wool nepps and yellow, green and blue Angelina.

2 Prepare your backing felt following the instructions on page 44. Roughly card together some light blue and white merino, and lay this down on the top third of your background. Graduate the colour so that the sky becomes lighter towards the bottom.

3 Lay a wavy strip of green merino across the bottom of the blue – this will form a distant line of hills. Try to create an organic shape that dips slightly in the middle, and don't worry if one side is thinner than the other.

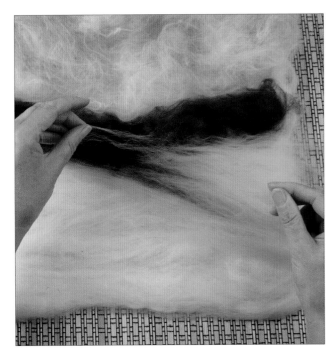

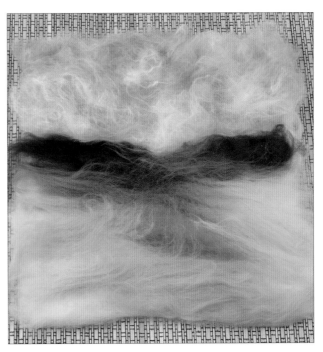

4 Tease out some pale green fibres and lay these below the dark green, overlapping the edges slightly so that the colours appear to blend together.

5 Continue to build up your foreground using thinly teased areas of different greens – in general make the colours lighter as you move down. Rather than working in horizontal bands of colour, create organic, broad strokes.

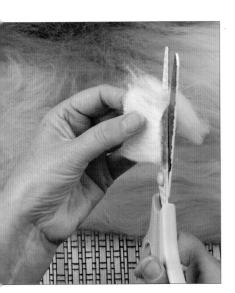

6 From an even chunk of white merino, cut out some rectangles to form your buildings. Position them as shown, so that they sit just just right of centre, on top of the light green fibres applied in step 4.

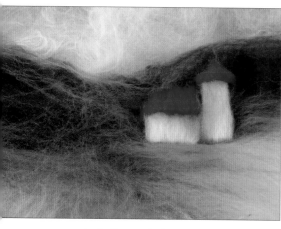

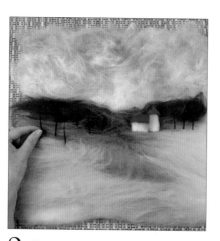

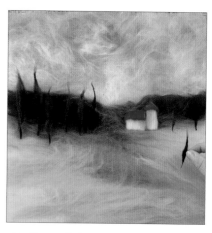

7 Cut roof shapes from red merino and place these on top of your buildings. Cut a few wisps of orange merino and place them on the join between the two buildings.

8 To create tree trunks, tightly twist some short strands of black merino and roughly position them along the base of the hills. The number you make is up to you – in this example, nine were used.

9 From dark green merino, create elegant tree shapes by cutting elongated leaf-like shapes and tightly twisting the ends. Place these on top of the tree trunks.

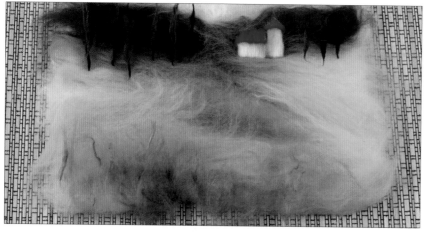

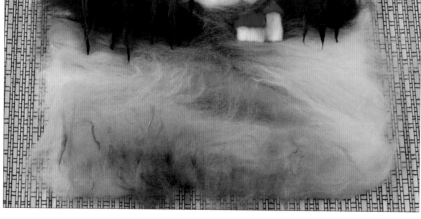

10 Cut some green silk fibres and position them in the foreground along the bottom of the picture. Vary the height of the fibres, and don't try to get them straight – wavy lines look much more natural.

11 Sprinkle a few green wool nepps around the tops of the green silk fibres.

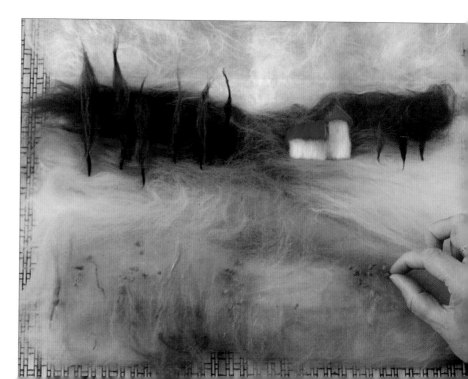

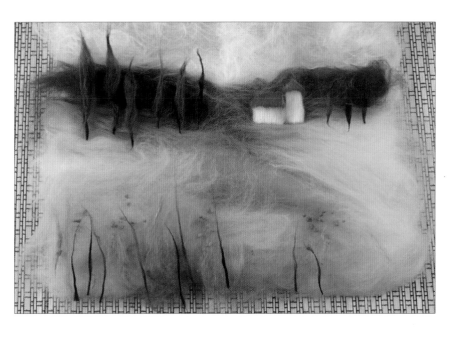

12 To add more detail to the foreground, twist some thin strands of green and black merino of various lengths. Position these along the bottom of the picture.

13 Take a chunk of bright yellow merino in one hand and using a pair of scissors snip off small chunks so that they fall onto the green area of the picture.

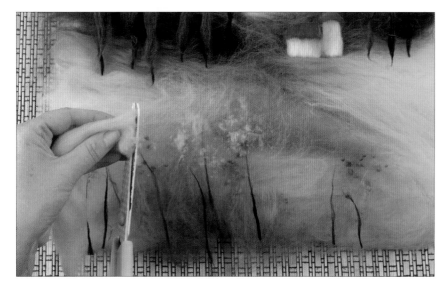

14 Continue to snip off chunks of yellow merino until the green area is speckled with yellow.

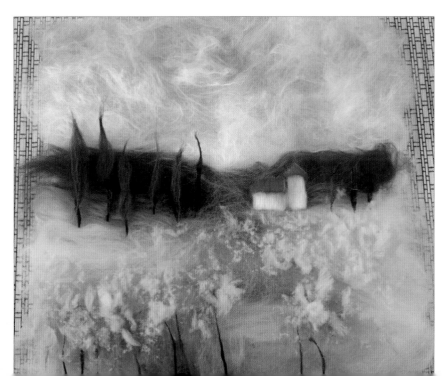

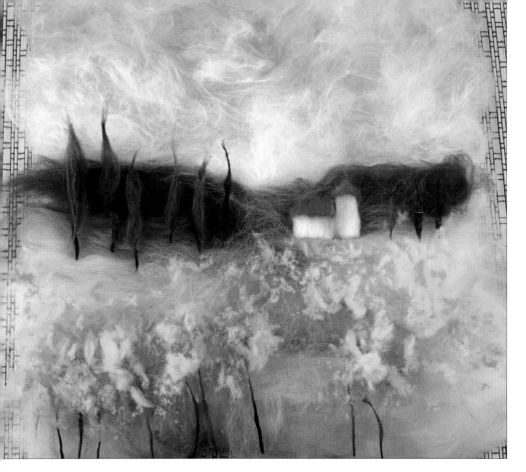

15 Repeat step 13, this time using orange merino. Cut finer, smaller pieces so that you do not overwhelm the yellow – the orange will give some depth to the picture and should therefore be more subtle.

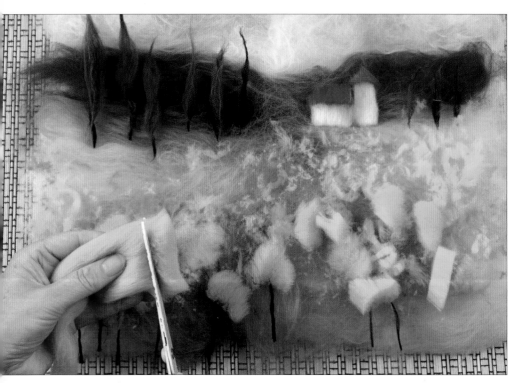

16 Repeat step 13, this time cutting large chunks of yellow merino. Concentrate these on the foreground of your picture. These largest chunks of yellow will form the most detailed sunflower heads. Carefully move and reposition them if you need to, to get the best arrangement.

17 Cut small pieces of brown merino, and place in the centres of your largest sunflowers.

18 Roll together some light and dark green merino fibres, then repeat step 13, trimming the green pieces over the very bottom of the picture and between some of the largest flowerheads.

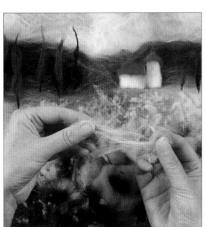

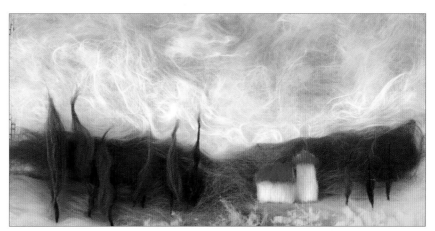

19 Tease out some very fine wisps of white silk and position these above the hill line to create glistening clouds. Create swirling, cloud-like shapes using the silk, tucking it behind the tops of the tallest trees.

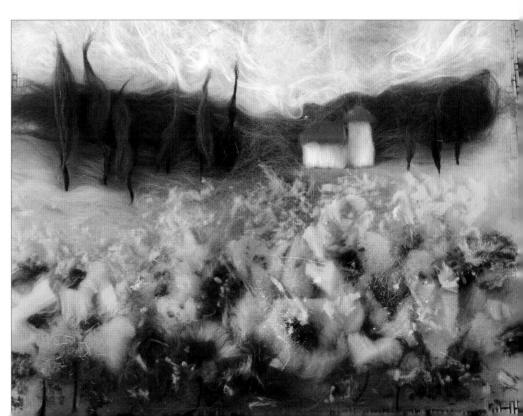

20 Finish the picture with some Angelina fibres: trim yellow fibres over the flowerheads, green fibres over the leaves, and blue fibres over the sky. You might want to add a few wispy black horizontal fibres along the bottom of the tree trunks. Wet felt following the instructions on pages 52–54.

Needle felting

21 Use the felting needle to reshape any areas that may have moved or become misshapen. Push the fibres into the correct position and stab through with the needle. Add a thin line of dark brown between the two buildings.

22 Tease out some thin wisps of dark brown merino and add these to the left hand side of the roof – apply a fine line of brown right the way around the edge of each roof.

23 Needle felt the tips of the trees in position so that they are upright, thin and pointed.

Machine stitching

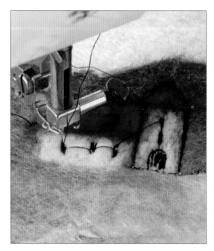 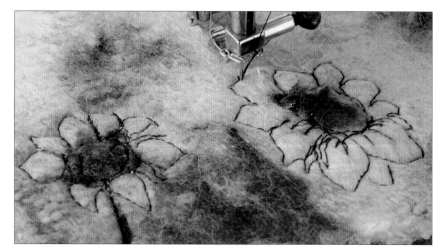

24 Prepare your machine for free machine embroidery with black thread in the top and in the bobbin. Draw in five windows and a small rounded door, then outline the entire building.

25 In the centre foreground 'draw' sunflower petals around a few of the brown areas – create jagged, sketchy rings of petals and sew a few wiggling lines over the brown centres. Here I created two complete flowers, but your picture will look different after the felting process, so create more or fewer depending on what you feel looks best.

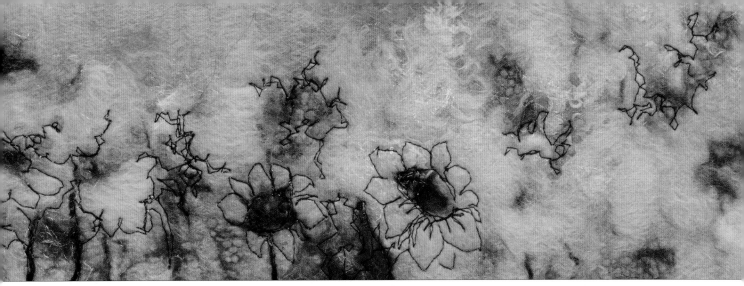

26 Continue to sew in the sunflowers, but as you move outwards and further up the picture, sew in gradually less detail. It can be very effective to draw in the negative spaces between the flowers, using sharp, wiggling lines to give a suggestion of their outlines – choose areas of green that are bordered with yellow and sew around the edges of the green.

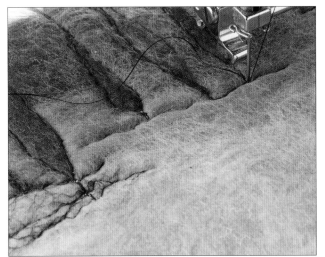

27 Outline the trees, then sew short horizontal lines under groups of two or three of them, connecting the bottoms of the trunks. Also sew a horizontal line under the buildings and continue it over to the right hand edge of the picture, following the light green horizon line – stop and lift the needle to sew past each of the trees.

28 Rethread your machine with green top and bobbin thread and sew a few parallel lines of stitching up the right hand side of each tree.

29 Rethread your machine with orange thread and sew in some detail on the two roofs: on the larger, wider roof, sew small vertical lines or triangles of stitching to give the impression of texture; cover half of the small, triangular roof with dense orange stitching.

Hand stitching

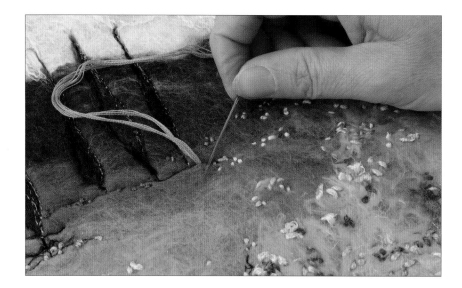

30 To create the illusion of lots of tiny glistening flowers, add small stitches in red, yellow, orange, white and green all over the picture.

31 Use dark brown embroidery silk to sew along the roof top, creating a few downward stitches on the roof, then block in the left side of the triangular roof. Use an orange silk to add a few more stitches to the right hand side of the triangular roof, to make it look three-dimensional.

32 For your large sunflowers, sew a few yellow stitches along the length of the petals then sew small, brown stitches on top of the centre. Use these two stitches to create the illusion of flowers all across the lower foreground, but don't be too exact with your stitching and only use a few stitches to suggest each flower.

Finishing

Finish your picture using the guidance on page 61.

INDEX

Tulips (close-up)

26 x 16cm (10¹⁄₂ x 6in)

This is one of the first flower feltings I created in 2002, yet remains one of my favourites. It has a very simple, almost abstract quality to it, with areas of stitching defining the form of the tulips.

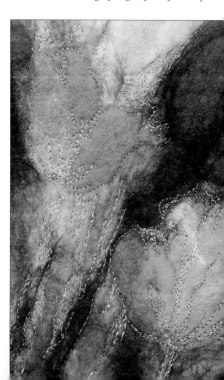

128